Cicero *Pro Roscio Amerino*

The following titles are available from Bloomsbury for the OCR specifications in Latin and Greek

Cicero *pro Roscio Amerino*: A Selection, with introduction, commentary notes and vocabulary by Neil Treble

OCR Anthology for Latin AS and A Level Shorter Prose Authors, covering the prescribed texts by Nepos, Tacitus and Apuleius, with introduction, commentary notes and vocabulary by Katharine Radice and Stuart R. Thomson

OCR Anthology for Latin AS and A Level Shorter Verse, covering the prescribed texts by Lucretius, Tibullus and Ovid, with introduction, commentary notes and vocabulary by John Godwin

OCR Anthology for Latin GCSE 2027–2028, covering the prescribed texts by Pliny the Younger, Aulus Gellius, Apuleius, Ovid and Virgil, with introduction, commentary notes and vocabulary by Tim Chambers and Declan Lawell

OCR Anthology for Classical Greek GCSE 2027–2028, covering the prescribed texts by Herodotus, Lysias, Homer and Euripides, with introduction, commentary notes and vocabulary by Christopher Burnand and Andy Mylne

OCR Anthology for Classical Greek AS and A Level: 2026–2028, covering the prescribed texts by Aristophanes, Herodotus, Homer, Lucian, Plato and Sophocles, with introduction, commentary notes and vocabulary by Matthew Barr, John Claughton, Benedict Gravell, Rowena Hewes, Ellice Hetherington and Stuart R. Thomson

Virgil *Aeneid* IV: A Selection, with introduction, commentary notes and vocabulary by John Storey

Supplementary resources for these volumes can be found at https://bloomsbury.pub/OCR-editions-2026-2028
Please type the URL into your web browser and follow the instructions to access the Companion Website.
If you experience any problems, please contact Bloomsbury at onlineresources@bloomsbury.com

Cicero *Pro Roscio Amerino*: A Selection

Sections 5–32, 37–57

With introduction, commentary notes and vocabulary by Neil Treble

BLOOMSBURY ACADEMIC
Bloomsbury Publishing Plc
50 Bedford Square, London, WC1B 3DP, UK
1385 Broadway, New York, NY 10018, USA
29 Earlsfort Terrace, Dublin 2, Ireland

BLOOMSBURY, BLOOMSBURY ACADEMIC and the Diana logo are trademarks of Bloomsbury Publishing Plc

First published in Great Britain 2025

Copyright © Neil Treble, 2025

Neil Treble has expressed his right under the Copyright, Designs and Patents Act, 1988, to be identified as Author of this work.

Cover design: Terry Woodley
Cover image: Roman mosaic in Carmona, Spain
© Manakin/istockphoto.com

All rights reserved. No part of this publication may be reproduced or transmitted in any form or by any means, electronic or mechanical, including photocopying, recording, or any information storage or retrieval system, without prior permission in writing from the publishers.

Bloomsbury Publishing Plc does not have any control over, or responsibility for, any third-party websites referred to or in this book. All internet addresses given in this book were correct at the time of going to press. The author and publisher regret any inconvenience caused if addresses have changed or sites have ceased to exist, but can accept no responsibility for any such changes.

A catalogue record for this book is available from the British Library.

A catalog record for this book is available from the Library of Congress.

ISBN:	PB:	978-1-3503-8445-3
	ePDF:	978-1-3503-8446-0
	eBook:	978-1-3503-8447-7

Typeset by RefineCatch Limited, Bungay, Suffolk
Printed and bound in Great Britain

To find out more about our authors and books visit www.bloomsbury.com and sign up for our newsletters.

Contents

Preface	vii
Introduction	1
Text	35
Commentary Notes	49
Vocabulary	127

Endorsement statement

The teaching content of this resource is endorsed by OCR for use with specification AS Level Latin (H043) and specification A Level Latin (H443).

All references to assessment, including assessment preparation and practice questions of any format/style are the publisher's interpretation of the specification and are not endorsed by OCR.

This resource was designed for use with the version of the specification available at the time of publication. However, as specifications are updated over time, there may be contradictions between the resource and the specification, therefore please use the information on the latest specification and Sample Assessment Materials at all times when ensuring students are fully prepared for their assessments.

Endorsement indicates that a resource is suitable to support delivery of an OCR specification, but it does not mean that the endorsed resource is the only suitable resource to support delivery, or that it is required or necessary to achieve the qualification.

OCR recommends that teachers consider using a range of teaching and learning resources based on their own professional judgement for their students' needs. OCR has not paid for the production of this resource, nor does OCR receive any royalties from its sale. For more information about the endorsement process, please visit the OCR website.

Preface

The text and notes in this volume aim to be a guide to any student wishing to advance beyond GCSE level Latin and, in doing so, to read a selection of passages from Cicero's powerful *Pro Sex. Roscio Amerino*.

This edition is particularly designed to support those who have undertaken to read the prescription of the speech set for examination as part of the Prose Literature component of OCR's AS Level and A Level Latin in the years 2026–8.

Pro Sex. Roscio Amerino is the earliest criminal case undertaken by Cicero in a long and distinguished career. As such, it provides real insight into the character and style of the orator who would become, perhaps, the most famous of the ancient world. While not as refined as some of his later speeches, Cicero's raw talent and technique, even at this early stage, are clear and foreshadow his future greatness and impact on both the legal and political scene in Rome. It must have been striking to those present to see the young, inexperienced Cicero take on such a case. The speech also gives us an understanding of the atmosphere created by the Sullan regime and the violence which accompanied it. Family members turn on family members for financial and political advantage and a shadowy member of the elite, using political and judicial weapons for personal advantage, lurks in the background. All the while, Cicero works carefully to avoid making himself a target for the regime. It is courtroom drama at its most captivating.

This volume's introduction aims to provide a clear summary of the life of Cicero while grounding the speech in the turbulent context of the Late Republic, the recent dictatorship of Sulla, and the political violence which had taken place. It also seeks to explore the charge which was brought against Sextus Roscius, the political dimensions of the case, and the possible punishment in the event of a guilty verdict. There is also a brief exploration of the system of courts in ancient Rome and the approach which Cicero takes when defending his client. In addition, a summary of Ciceronian style aims to help students appreciate the techniques he uses to intensify the power of his arguments throughout the speech.

The commentary notes support students as they move between GCSE and AS / A Level, highlighting the more complex points of grammar, assisting with structure and word order and providing suggested translations for idiomatic words and phrases. Further cultural and historical information is also provided in the commentary notes as seemed appropriate, as well as notes highlighting key points of style and rhetorical technique for students. Summaries of some sections of the speech not included in the prescription are also included where it was felt these would elucidate students' understanding. Students reading the speech as a Group 2 text should be aware that sections 35–36 and 58–78 should also be read in English when studying for the A Level.

Additional supporting material can also be found on the website including quizzes, an electronic version of the text and a full timeline of Cicero's life to aid students in their study of the text.

At the end of the book, a full vocabulary list is included, with words also found in OCR's Defined Vocabulary List for AS Level Latin marked with an asterisk.

The text in this edition follows E. H. Donkin's *Bristol Classical Press* (2006 edition) with minor amendments as seemed appropriate.

I would like to thank Alice Wright and her team at Bloomsbury for their help and support (and flexibility with deadlines), but mostly for the opportunity to work on this particular text. I have been teaching Cicero to A Level students since the beginning of my career and, as Cicero's first criminal case, to spend such a sustained time with *Pro Sex. Roscio Amerino* was a real delight.

I hope students will find it as exciting, impassioned and dynamic a start to his career as I do.

Neil Treble
30 June 2024

Introduction

Cicero's life

To many outside the study of Classics, the name Cicero probably means very little. Ask them to name a Roman and most will likely plump for Julius Caesar, some perhaps for Augustus. Even Marcus Crassus, through his starring role in Horrible Histories' *Minted Song*, has gained some notoriety as Rome's richest man. But Cicero has, somehow, failed to make it into the collective consciousness in quite the same way.

When it comes down to it, while it is fair to say Cicero's military achievements pale into insignificance set against Caesar's, and his political impact is certainly less than that of Augustus, the legacy which he has left resonates, though less obviously, through the ages with an impact which is perhaps just as great as those of his better-known contemporaries. To students of the Classical world, this is even more so. While Caesar left his commentaries on the various wars undertaken in Gaul, Spain and elsewhere, and Augustus left us his *Res Gestae*, a catalogue of achievements from his thirty-one-year reign as *princeps*, Cicero left us a mountain of material which informs our understanding of Rome in the first century BC made up of speeches, letters and philosophy.

It is the first two of these, the speeches and letters, which serve as our major tool in understanding the seismic changes which took place in Rome during the period of Cicero's life. In fact, the OCR A Level Ancient History textbook, *The Breakdown of the Late Republic*, goes as far as pointing out specifically the scarcity of contemporary source material relating to the period after Cicero's death. The speeches came in two forms, legal or political (of which this speech, *Pro Sex. Roscio Amerino*, falls, perhaps, into both camps, being primarily a speech about the murder of Roscius' father delivered in court but with a distinctly political thread woven through it).

Cicero's legal speeches demonstrate the manner in which Roman advocates navigated Rome's legal system, what methods were acceptable to defend their clients or prosecute their opponents. Many of Cicero's speeches, the majority in defence of his client, are considered masterpieces of ancient rhetoric, showcasing the very best of oratorical technique and many are still studied today by students of rhetoric and politicians looking to imitate Cicero's style. His political speeches, often given at moments of great crisis in the Republic (*In Catilinam*, the *Philippics*), not only further showcase Cicero's style but give us significant insight into the workings of these pivotal events in Rome's history. Undoubtedly, these were polished for publication after the event and one can never be absolutely sure which words were actually delivered on the occasion but, as far as eyewitness testimony from an active participant in the political events of the time goes, Cicero wins hands down.

His letters, likewise, are a goldmine of material relating to both the politics and domestic life of the time. Many are written to other political figures of the time expressing Cicero's thoughts on important matters, some to friends (a large number to his long-time friend, Atticus) which explore political topics but also more day-to-day matters such as relations between family members and even practical matters like the upkeep of Cicero's various villas and the refurbishment of his library. The letters written during the time of Cicero's exile paint a picture of a man broken and potentially suicidal, while those written about his daughter, Tullia, show a man full of love, concern and regret. Even his faithful slave and secretary, Tiro, features showing the possible (although undoubtedly rare) depths of affection between master and slave.

Cicero's political achievements (of which there are many) may not match the fame and glory of some of his rivals and, undoubtedly, he failed to spot the changing political tide of the first century BC but, without him and his significant body of work, our understanding of the political world of Republican Rome would be vastly diminished.

Early life

Cicero, unlike many of his contemporaries, was not Roman by birth. Instead, he hailed from Arpinum (modern Arpino), a town about sixty miles south-east of the city (and likely not dissimilar to Ameria, the hometown of Sextus Roscius). When Cicero was born in 106 BC the citizens of Arpinum did not have full rights as Roman citizens, only gaining these in 90 BC after the Social War (between Rome and its allies) when Arpinum was declared a municipium. This fact undoubtedly dogged Cicero for much of his political life as, by many in political circles, he was considered an outsider ('and if it suits for you and me to be considered foreigners by the other patricians...', *Pro Sulla* 25). Similarly, his family was not one of the great political dynasties of the Roman Republic, having no men who had achieved senatorial rank among his family members. On his entry into politics, therefore, Cicero was a *novus homo* (*new man*) distinguishing him from the more prominent patrician and aristocratic senators who considered their influence an inalienable right by birth and the legacy of their ancestors. The arrival of interlopers such as Cicero only, in their minds, diminished this status and their *dignitas*.

Nevertheless, Cicero's father, a member of the local nobility in Arpinum, determined that an education in Rome was necessary for Cicero and his younger brother (Quintus Cicero) and, likely having been educated at home in Arpinum, both were taken to Rome in the 90s BC to receive a level of training which would prepare them for entry into the political life of the city. Cicero was apprenticed to men of considerable rank and influence who would allow him to experience the cut and thrust of Rome's politics, spending time in the homes of the noted orators Lucius Licinius Crassus and Marcus Antonius, the grandfather of his eventual rival of the same name.

In 91 BC, one of the great issues of the first century BC exploded into violence and war. The question of citizenship rights among Rome's allies had been a long-standing issue and, when a tribune attempted to pass a law providing citizenship to Rome's allies and this was rejected, Rome's allies rose in revolt. During this time Cicero undertook military service under the commander Sulla (who would eventually become dictator of Rome) but did not particularly take to soldiering and, after a period of service, returned to Rome and his training in preparation for entering public life. That moment was delayed further, however, by the outbreak of civil war between the Marian and Sullan factions and the establishment of a populist regime at Rome under Marius and his ally Cinna which, according to Plutarch, caused Cicero to withdraw into the life of a scholar and philosopher.

By 82 BC Sulla had returned from a campaign in the East and seized power in Rome, establishing a brutal dictatorship which used fear to maintain order. The establishment of this fear was based, to a large extent on the use of proscriptions (the declaration of an individual as a public enemy resulting in summary execution without judicial process and the confiscation of their property) but by the end of 81 BC Sulla had reorganized the political system in Rome, re-established the courts and declared himself a candidate for the consulship of 80 BC, relinquishing the dictatorship. The moment for Cicero to make his entrance into public life had arrived.

The beginnings of his legal and political career

The speech *Pro Sex. Roscio Amerino* is not the first extant speech we have by Cicero. *Pro Publio Quinctio* a civil case concerning a property dispute between Publius Quinctius and a business associate of his brother has come down to us intact and, within, Cicero also makes references to other cases he had made in the courts (*Pro Publio Quinctio* 4). 80 BC and the speech in defence of Roscius is, however, significant in that it is the first criminal case undertaken by Cicero. The case was risky (see below) and Cicero showed courage taking it on when others had clearly refused to do so. The stakes were equally balanced by the possible rewards, and the public interest in the case catapulted Cicero to fame when he won it. The reputation he had gained brought him significant numbers of new cases but, interestingly, Cicero chose this moment to take a break and continue his study of oratory abroad heading to Athens and Rhodes in 79 BC, claiming the strain through his style of speaking demonstrated the need to work on his technique. Plutarch claims that fear of Sulla caused Cicero to leave but, considering the date of Cicero's departure (and that Sulla died in 79 BC while Cicero remained abroad until 77 BC), this seems unlikely.

Rise through the ranks

On his return to Rome in 77 BC, Cicero prepared for election to office, standing in the elections of 76 BC for the office of quaestor. He was successful and was sent to Sicily for the year 75 BC where he was made responsible for the grain supply. His return to Rome saw his successful prosecution of the governor of Sicily, Gaius Verres, for corruption in 70 BC, the same year in which he was elected to the office of aedile for 69 BC. There followed a campaign for the office of praetor which he held in 66 BC (overseeing the extortion court in Rome) and, while doing so, he courted the support of the noted general Pompeius Magnus (Pompey the Great). Cicero's rise through the ranks was swift and impressive, particularly given the disadvantages of his background as *the man from Arpinum* and a *novus homo*.

Consulship

There was now only one office of the *cursus honorum* (the system of political offices in Rome) which Cicero had not held: the consulship. His campaign for the position was well planned and executed (a handbook of electioneering, *Commentariolum Petitionis*, perhaps written by Cicero's brother Quintus, survives from the time, showing the depth of thinking which went into the campaign) and Cicero was successful. When he took up the consulship for 63 BC with his colleague, Antonius Hybrida, Cicero had obtained each of the offices of state coming from a family of no political background in the first year in which he was eligible to do so. This was an incredible rarity for a man in his position and a testament to the political prowess he demonstrated. He himself was particularly proud that he had been elected to the consulship by the unanimous support of the voting centuries in the assembly.

The triumvirate and withdrawal from public life

In many ways, however, Cicero peaked too soon. He was never to be consul again, despite his young age in the scheme of Roman politics. He established a political principle which he termed *concordia ordinum* ('harmony of the orders') suggesting stability and cooperation between the various classes of individual in the city was what would bring prosperity and was lauded by many for his actions during the Catiline Conspiracy which took place during the winter of 63 BC, receiving the title of *pater patriae* ('father of the fatherland'). Nevertheless, it was clear that he had made enemies and the act of putting conspirators to death without trial (even at the behest of the vast majority of the senate) had given these enemies ammunition. His customary speech at the end of his consulship was vetoed by a tribune, the populist movement found momentum in the First Triumvirate, an informal pact between Julius Caesar, Pompeius Magnus and Marcus Crassus, which arose late 60 BC / early 59 BC and allowed the three to dominate political events at Rome. Cicero, admirably but perhaps foolishly refused to involve himself with the three. By 58 BC Cicero found himself isolated and without support and vulnerable, resulting in the passing of a decree by a political enemy, Clodius, which demanded his exile. Cicero would spend the next year or so far from Rome in Greece. On his return, attempts to involve himself in Rome's politics were met with threats from the Triumvirate and he found himself supporting Caesar against his will, an act he regretted later. Gradually Cicero withdrew into philosophy, producing both *De Oratore* ('On the Orator') and *De Re Publica* ('On the Republic') during this period while lamenting what he perceived to be the loss of the Republic.

Civil war and assassination

The events of the 40s BC to some extent revitalized Cicero and allowed him to become the elder statesman which he had expected to become after his rapid rise to power in the 60s BC. The Triumvirate broke down, firstly with the death of Crassus (53 BC) while on campaign against the Parthians, and then when Caesar crossed the Rubicon (January 49 BC) as a result of increasing tension between him and his erstwhile partner Pompeius who had now aligned himself with the senate. Cicero sided with Pompeius in the resulting civil war which he, and his Republican forces, lost allowing Caesar to take the role of dictator and supreme power in Rome. Unlike Sulla, Caesar had no intention of relinquishing the powers granted to him and, having been declared dictator three times already, each for an increased period, he was eventually declared *dictator in perpetuum* ('dictator for life') in February 44 BC. A plot was formed and he was assassinated on the Ides of March 44 BC.

Cicero was, by Roman standards, now an old man (around sixty-two years of age) and had not been involved in the plot against Caesar. Nevertheless, he saw the opportunity for a final push to save the Republic from the tyranny which had controlled it for the last decade. He set about organizing the conspirators (or liberators as they viewed themselves) and, most importantly, set out to attack Marcus Antonius (a key associate of Caesar) through a series of speeches known as the *Philippics* in which Cicero held nothing back, savaging Antonius with invective against his lifestyle, morals, sexuality, drunkenness and general political ineptitude. As in 63 BC, however, it seems Cicero had misjudged the situation and the strength of his hand. Antonius paired with Caesar's heir, Octavian (later to become the emperor Augustus) and with Marcus Lepidus (Caesar's *magister equitum* ('master of the horse'), a deputy of sorts) to form the Second Triumvirate, this time a formally recognized political office. The three made extensive use of proscriptions, just as Sulla had done, to eliminate their enemies and to raise funds through confiscation of property. Antonius, enraged by Cicero's treatment of him in his *Philippics*, insisted that Cicero be included in the list of those to be killed (Augustus would later claim that he had resisted) and Cicero was murdered in December 43 BC while on the run from his villa at Caieta by soldiers acting for the Triumvirate.

Cicero's head and hands were displayed on the rostra (speaker's platform) in the forum at Rome and Antonius' wife, Fulvia, is said to have pierced the dead Cicero's tongue as an act of vengeance against the man who had spoken so viciously against her husband. It is thanks to Cicero's friend Atticus and his slave Tiro (who catalogued and arranged Cicero's speeches and letters for publication) that Cicero's legacy lives on and his life provides the mass of source material for students of the period that we have available to us. That, and the enduring power of Cicero's rhetorical style which has given it an appeal unrivalled in Latin literature.

The case

The accusation of murder

On the face of things, the charge is pretty simple. Sextus Roscius the Younger is accused of the murder of his father (known as *parricidium*), Sextus Roscius the Elder, by two other members of the family, Magnus and Capito. There are, however, a number of complicating factors.

The background of the elder Roscius and the circumstances of his death

The elder Roscius, father of Cicero's client, was an extremely wealthy man with enormous assets. As such, he was regularly in Rome and often stayed in the city. He was, therefore, extremely well known in Rome's social circles and recognizable to some members of the Roman elite. His murder took place in Rome one night on the return from a dinner party. The prosecution takes an approach that is termed *cui bono* ('who benefits'), arguing that the younger Roscius had motive because of the great wealth which he was likely to inherit upon his death. The obvious counter to this, as employed by Cicero, is that the younger Roscius did not in fact inherit the estates (as we shall explore later) and that he was not in Rome at the time of the murder.

Proscription

After the elder Roscius' death, it was discovered that his name had been entered onto a proscription list. This tool had been used throughout Sulla's dictatorship to eliminate political enemies and to confiscate their property. The property would then be sold at auction for the benefit of the state. The lists themselves had been closed since 81 BC meaning that for a whole year the elder Roscius had been living his life as an enemy of the state. Despite the suspicious nature of these circumstances, the elder Roscius' property was indeed confiscated and sold at public auction meaning that the younger Roscius gained nothing from his death. There are three major points here, two which Cicero seizes upon and another which he ignores. Firstly, the elder Roscius, so Cicero declares, was a known advocate of the Sullan regime. What motivation did the regime possibly have to silence a supporter?

Secondly, being proscribed was not something to be taken lightly. The names of those declared enemies of the state were published openly and those who found their names on a list immediately forfeited their property rights, their citizenship (including their right to trial) and could expect to be killed on sight. Those who acted on the proscription order would anticipate material benefit from doing so, giving great incentive to turn on those around you in the event that a family member's name appeared on one of the lists. At the height of the disturbances during the 80s BC, friends, slaves and close relatives had all been known to take advantage of proscriptions of people close to them. As a result, individuals who were proscribed took every possible step to protect themselves by going into hiding or, more likely, going into exile. The elder Roscius did neither of these two things, instead living the very public life that he had done so previously. It seems neither he nor those around him were aware of the proscription (an impossible state of affairs considering the very public nature of the declarations).

Finally, and, for whatever reason, Cicero chooses not to pursue this argument, given the incentive for family members to turn on their own when one among them was proscribed, there is some question as to whether, in this instance, the younger Roscius could be found guilty of killing a man who had been proscribed, even his father. The entire basis for the case, therefore, seems somewhat confused. There is a possibility that Cicero felt this was not a line which could be easily argued (as it tries to swerve the question of guilt vs innocence) and that he should instead defend the charge sincerely rather than seeking to question the legitimacy of the trial. Regardless, this inconsistency, particularly when combined with the lack of reaction from the elder Roscius, brings serious doubts as to the authenticity of the proscription.

Chrysogonus and the political dimension

As it stands, the circumstances seem suspicious enough. However, the political aspect of the case goes deeper than a rather unexpected and unknown proscription. The auction of the elder Roscius' property resulted in an equally suspicious outcome. The thirteen farms (perhaps think *estates*) which had an approximate value of 600,000 sesterces were sold for a mere 2,000 to a freedman by the name of Chrysogonus. The sum paid would have raised more than a few eyebrows, but the reason is obvious. Chrysogonus had been in the service of the dictator, Sulla, and through his position had gained enormous wealth, power and influence. Undoubtedly any other potential bidders were intimidated into silence during the auction, and Chrysogonus' status as part of Sulla's household allowed him to snap up a bargain. By extension, there is a clear possibility that the elder Roscius was proscribed with this outcome in mind. Furthermore, the people of Ameria had been so outraged that the local senators (the *decuriones*) passed a resolution to send a delegation to Sulla himself who was, at that time, at his camp at Volaterrae, and request that the elder Roscius' name be removed from the proscription list and the younger Roscius have his inheritance restored to him. The delegation was met by Chrysogonus who made assurances that the request would be presented to Sulla. No further action appears to have been taken except for the charge being brought against the younger Roscius. One might hypothesize that Chrysogonus felt the objections of the Amerians would lessen if the younger Roscius had himself been disposed of. For an advocate defending the younger Roscius, therefore, Chrysogonus' political influence and his close association with the Sullan regime mean that any arguments presented need to tread a careful line between defence of the charge and attacking the regime by inference.

The relationship between the elder Roscius and Magnus and Capito

The relationship between the elder Roscius and those bringing the charge, Titus Roscius Magnus and Titus Roscius Capito, was, Cicero suggests, subject to a long-standing family feud relating to property. When the murder of the elder Roscius occurred, word was sent from Rome by Magnus to Ameria (via a courier called Mallius Glaucia). Magnus chose not to send word to the elder Roscius' son, however, but directed Glaucia to inform Capito of what had happened. If one were to ask who benefitted from the crime, the finger would surely have to point at Magnus and Capito. Magnus was appointed steward of ten of the farms on behalf of Chrysogonus while Capito was gifted the remaining three. It is a brave, or foolish, man who tries to unravel the emerging web of connections between Magnus, Capito and Chrysogonus without implicating Sulla himself in the affair.

The punishment for the charge and the political environment of the time

As well as the complex and, potentially, politically dangerous nature of the case, the wider political and legal situation of the recent years and the very nature of the charge also meant defending Sextus Roscius carried significant risks. Due to the political turmoil of the 80s BC, the courts had been closed for a period of time, and Sulla had introduced significant reform to the judicial system as part of his attempts to stabilize Rome. This meant that Cicero's case would be heard by a panel of senators, not equestrians as would previously have been the case, potentially heightening the political aspects of the case. Much more important, however, is that, with the courts having been closed, this was the first case of *parricidium* to be heard in recent times. The charge itself would always have attracted significant interest due to the quasi-religious nature of the crime (to a Roman, the murder of one's father was essentially a crime against the gods, reverence and respect for one's father being the expected mode of behaviour), but this interest was undoubtedly multiplied by the extreme nature of the crime after a period of judicial inactivity. Certainly the prosecution team felt that the odds were in their favour: for a crime of this nature, the expectation would be a guilty verdict and the condemnation of the younger Roscius. Cicero undoubtedly started with a serious disadvantage.

Furthermore, because of the serious nature of the crime, the Romans maintained the use of an archaic, ritualistic, system of punishment which, it was felt, suitably reflected the outrage committed by one who murders a parent.

On pronouncement of the guilty verdict, it is suggested that:

- the condemned would be covered with a wolf's pelt and have wooden sandals bound to his feet;
- he would then be beaten with rods and forced to enter a leather sack into which were also placed a dog, a cockerel, a viper and a monkey;
- the sack and its contents would finally be thrown into a body of water (presumably the Tiber in Rome) which would then be left to sink and for those inside to drown.

Each aspect of this extremely elaborate and cruel punishment has some religious or symbolic aspect to it. The wolf's pelt (which covered the condemned's face) and the wooden shoes perhaps prevented him from polluting the air and the ground with his breath and touch. The animals were chosen for their symbolism (dogs were hated in the Roman world, cockerels were said to have no affection for their parents, vipers and other snakes were universally despised and monkeys were considered base forms of humans), and the choice of water as a final resting place created a seal around the condemned, separating them from the rest of the world.

The precise details are the subject of debate – Cicero makes direct mention of the sack in the speech but no mention of any animals either here or in any other work where he refers to the topic. There are also objections that Roman courts did not sentence individuals to death, merely fines or exile, and that other mentions of this grim punishment usually infer that it was not likely to be used. Unlikely as it may have been, therefore, that this punishment was ever a realistic prospect in the Roscius case (even in the event of a guilty verdict Roscius probably would have fled Rome and gone into self-imposed exile before the punishment could be carried out), the mere threat of it and the excitement surrounding the slightest possibility that a man could be subjected to such an extreme form of execution would likely have created significant public interest. For Cicero, this is a double-edged sword: greater interest means a boosted public profile but, conversely, the stakes also become higher and the fall that much greater if he were to lose the case.

The Roman court system

It is worthwhile thinking briefly about the environment in which Roscius' case would be tried. The Roman court system had grown from a system of popular courts (where the case would be heard in front of the entire citizen body) to a system of judicial courts, established in 149 BC, where cases would be overseen by a presiding magistrate (in the Roscius trial, a praetor Marcus Fannius) along with a jury of around fifty individuals whose role it was to examine the arguments, reach a decision concerning the guilt of the defendant and propose a suitable punishment. This was a much more reasonable proposition since Rome's citizen body had expanded significantly during the period of the Republic and, by Cicero's day, the vast majority of cases (although not all) were decided by a panel of jurors.

However, many of the features of the former popular court system remained. There was no public prosecution system, so individuals had to lodge their case with the presiding magistrate and either present their case themselves or appoint an advocate to plead the case on their behalf. In this case, Magnus and Capito employed the service of a highly experienced prosecutor called Erucius (although, despite his skill, Erucius' background gave Cicero sufficient ammunition to attack him directly). Similarly, the defendant could present their own defence or appoint a lawyer to act on his behalf. In theory, neither advocate was paid although the publicity gained was a particular draw for an aspiring politician like Cicero and, undoubtedly, arrangements were made for remuneration along with favours and legacies promised to successful advocates.

After Sulla's reforms of the judicial system, there were eight standing courts in Rome, each dealing with distinct forms of criminal activity (e.g. bribery, injury, counterfeiting) and each with a praetor overseeing their activities. Originally these courts would have been convened as inquests under the popular court system and so were still known by the name *quaestiones* ('investigations'). The trial of Roscius was brought before the *quaestio inter sicarios*, 'the court dealing with assassins', but which dealt with any case of murder. In addition, the Roscius case, because of the nature of the charge, could be taken *extra ordinem*, that is outside of the usual order. Normally cases would be heard sequentially based on the order in which they had been raised with a magistrate, but Roscius' case would have been shunted up the list going some way to explaining why this particular case was the first to be heard in this court since they reopened.

The prosecution and defence would then present their arguments in front of the panel which, again under Sulla's reforms intended to strengthen the senatorial order, could only be drawn from members of the senate. More importantly, however, and perhaps surprisingly by modern standards, the court was convened outside, in the open air of the forum. This reflected the manner of the popular courts which provided distraction and entertainment to the citizen body as well as an opportunity to engage in the judicial process. Arguments were presented, evidence offered, and witnesses called but, in part because of the environment of the court and the presence of the general public, a sense of legal proceedings as performance remained. Advocates would directly attack and smear their opponents, the circumstantial and improbable were included in arguments, witnesses were insulted and degraded by the opposing counsel, and the bar was low when it came to what was admissible as evidence. The mood of the crowd undoubtedly played a part in deciding outcomes (at times degenerating into riots in particularly contentious cases which caused trials to be abandoned) and, in the end, it was the rhetorical skill of one's lawyer (or often a team of lawyers) and the performance they gave which was the most significant factor in deciding the outcome of a case. Cicero himself is said to have admitted to obtaining acquittal for clients whom he knew to be guilty.

Cicero's approach to the case

Structure of the speech

The structure of classical rhetoric followed clearly defined patterns which allowed for a comprehensive examination of the issues. Many speeches from the ancient world, understandably, therefore, follow a structure which adheres to these relatively closely. For the most part following convention, Cicero's speech in defence of Sextus Roscius, is arranged as follows.

Introduction (exordium)*:*
Sections 1–13 (of which 5–13 in this edition)

> I have been chosen as the man most able to speak with the least risk, not chosen so that Sextus Roscius has the strongest possible defence, but so that he is not absolutely abandoned.
>
> Cicero, *Pro Sex. Roscio Amerino* 5

The introductions to Cicero's speeches are invariably striking, and this, his first criminal trial, is no exception. Cicero paints a picture of Roscius as helpless and abandoned, and of himself inexperienced but the only support available. At the same time, the case itself is presented not as a trial about the murder of Roscius' father, but as a fight for Roscius' life in the face of the powerful and corrupt Chrysogonus, a man who is willing to go to any lengths to get what he wants. That includes making the court a pawn in his games and using them as a tool to dispose of those who might challenge him. Fear features heavily: fear of those who refused to speak on Roscius' behalf out of considerations of their own safety, and the fear which Roscius feels for his own life. It is Roscius who has been wronged but stands accused while those who have wronged him prosecute him. The crowd may expect a guilty verdict but, by finding Roscius guilty, Cicero declares, the court becomes complicit in allowing murder to be committed with impunity.

The opening of the speech is filled with rhetorical flourish designed to manipulate the emotions of the jurors from the off. In particular, Cicero makes extensive use of *pathos* as a mode of argument both with reference to Roscius, a man utterly destroyed by what has happened to him, and to himself, the youthful, unpractised speaker, intimidated by the environment in which he finds himself and the great authority of the jurors. A liberal smattering of flattery towards Marcus Fannius (the praetor overseeing the court) and the other jurors is rounded off by the note of fear which he strikes about an imminent breakdown of law and order in the Republic which the events in this case foreshadow.

*Account of the facts (***narratio***):*
Sections 14-35 (of which 14-32 in this edition)

> While the younger Roscius had dedicated himself to the family estate and to a life in the country, Magnus himself was often at Rome, and Sextus Roscius was killed returning from dinner in the area of the baths at Pallacina.
>
> Cicero, *Pro Sex. Roscio Amerino* 18

The *narratio* seeks to lay out the facts as Cicero sees them. He deals with the life and background of the murdered man, Sextus Roscius the elder, and depicts a man of honour, with links to noble families and a supporter of the Sullan regime. An apparent breakdown of relations with Magnus and Capito also features, suggestive of ulterior motives in their bringing of the case. There follows an account of the murder and the events afterwards, all the time noting aspects of the details which should cause the jurors to be suspicious of the charge against the younger Roscius: the addition of the elder Roscius' name to the proscription list and the absurdly low figure paid for the purchase of his assets by Chrysogonus. Cicero also makes considerable mention of the delegation by the Amerians to Sulla (including the reading of a decree passed by the local magistrates), demonstrating clearly the strength of local opposition, and the assurance by Chrysogonus that the elder Roscius' name would be removed from the proscription lists, a clear sign of his corruptness, and the emergence of the plot to use the courts to remove the younger Roscius.

It is important to remember, however, that these are not *the facts* per se, but *the facts as Cicero saw them*, presented in a way which most helps his case and the defence of his client. We do not have an account of what was said by the prosecution lawyer, Erucius, and can only attempt to reconstruct his arguments from the way in which Cicero presents his defence. His depiction of the elder Roscius is designed to appeal to the sensibilities of a Roman audience, emphasizing those aspects of his character and conduct which they would consider virtues and designed to stand in contrast to his characterization of Magnus and Capito (cut-throat villains) and Chrysogonus (greedy and avaricious).

A summary of the arguments to follow (partitio)*:*
Sections 35–36 (not in this edition but to be read in
English if studying the Group 2 text for A Level)

> As far as I can tell, there are three matters which face Sextus Roscius at this time: the accusation made by his opponents, their audacity, and their power.
>
> Cicero, *Pro Sex. Roscio Amerino* 35

After the *narratio* it was standard form for an orator to take a moment to pause and present briefly the arguments which they intended to lay out in relation to the case, a section known as a *partitio* (or a *divisio*). The three aspects of the case which Cicero intends to argue (as shown above) are: the accusation itself, the audacity of his opponents, the power which they wield. Cicero takes this opportunity, however, to make each of these the responsibility of named individuals. The accusation he assigns to the prosecution lawyer, Erucius, immediately smearing him as a false accuser by describing the charge as a *confictio* (*invention*). Audacity he applies to Magnus and Capito while power he assigns to the hands of Chrysogonus. In doing so, he ensures that all parties are associated with negative qualities: Erucius is willing to concoct a prosecution for personal gain, Magnus and Capito show their willingness to play the system by spinning a tale of simply shocking proportions, and Chrysogonus uses his power and influence to corrupt the system.

Interestingly, Cicero also assigns the responsibility for confronting these challenges to named individuals. It is his responsibility to tackle the charge (in his capacity as Roscius' defence), but it is the responsibility of the jurors to tackle excessive audacity and the abuse of power. In doing so, Cicero presents a moral imperative for the jurors to acquit Roscius.

Examination of the accusation (propositio): *Sections 37–82 (Sections 37–57 in this edition, Sections 58–78 to be read in English if studying the Group 2 text for A Level)*

> So be it, you are not able to offer any motive. Even though I ought to have won outright, nevertheless, convinced of his innocence, I shall draw back from what is my right and make a concession to you which I would not make in another trial, I do not ask you why Sextus Roscius killed his father, I ask you how he did it.
>
> Cicero, *Pro Sex. Roscio Amerino* 73

When looking at the charge itself, Cicero focuses in on two main aspects, the motive the younger Roscius had for killing his father and the method for doing so. Cicero talks extensively about the motive and the lack of evidence which the prosecution has offered. Surely such a heinous act can only have been carried out by a man utterly devoid of all conscience? A man so broken by debts, lust and depravity that killing his father seemed the only way out? Erucius has, according to Cicero, already discounted these things: according to his evidence the younger Roscius lived a life in the country, did not even attend social gatherings and had no debts.

There are, again, two main strands to the prosecution argument concerning motive according to Cicero: (1) the younger Roscius was disliked by his father, and (2) he intended to disinherit him. Of the first, Cicero can find no evidence. It seems the prosecution have compared the treatment of the younger Roscius by his father with that of his, now deceased, brother. The brother was taken to Rome, attended parties and was by his father's side at all times while Cicero's client was left in Ameria to tend to the farms. Cicero does not view this as evidence of dislike but of the actions of a father who wishes to do the best by his son, entrusting him with the family estate and providing him with an environment which encourages clean living and virtue, drawing on historical precedent to support his argument. In terms of disinheritance, Cicero challenges Erucius to reveal why he thinks this was the case, countering by suggesting that there was no reason, that it did not happen, and that Erucius would be better fabricating something than offering so weak a justification.

When it comes to method, it seems the prosecution have offered almost nothing. Cicero offers a striking volley of questions (Section 74, not in this edition) – Did Roscius do the act himself? Did he employ others? If so, who? Were they free men or slaves? Where were they from? Where did he meet them? How did he persuade them?

If Cicero's rhetoric here is a genuine response to the evidence of the prosecution, it is not hard to see why he resorts to insult, attack and threats throughout this part of the speech. Erucius is taunted for his lack of understanding when it comes to father–son relations (being perhaps of uncertain parentage himself), his ability as a prosecutor is questioned and he is threatened with the consequences of false prosecution (branding and banning from prosecuting further cases). Cicero even draws on historical and mythical precedent to show the impact of *parricidium* on those who commit it and the seriousness with which the charge must be examined. He has not done so and, conversely, reacted with extreme discomfort when Cicero made mention of Chrysogonus. With, seemingly, so little to which to respond, it is clear that Cicero decided attack was undoubtedly the best form of defence.

Presentation of the defence (confirmatio): Sections 83–143 (not in this edition)

The *confirmatio*, Cicero's presentation of his own argument (rather than arguing against the prosecution's arguments), is split into two main sections. In these he himself turns prosecutor.

Attack on Magnus and Capito: Sections 83–123

> In Sextus Roscius, you will find no motive. But I do find one in Titus Roscius. For my focus is now on you, Titus Roscius, since you are sitting there and declare publicly that you are our enemy.
> Cicero, *Pro Sex. Roscio Amerino* 84

Cicero turns first against Magnus claiming he will deal with Capito later, but the focus is very much on the question of who benefitted (*cui bono*). Not only did Magnus benefit greatly from the elder Roscius' death, Cicero focuses on his previous situation, one of poverty. Who is more likely to have carried out the murder? The man who was an enemy and to whom the crime brought wealth, or the man who was the victim's son and now lives in destitution? Cicero then turns from the motive to the opportunity of carrying out the murder. Magnus was in Rome, the younger Roscius was not. Magnus was associated with other men of bad repute and under the protection of others. Roscius lived a life of solitude. It was an associate of Magnus who brought the news to Capito in Ameria and, what is more, he evidently did it at significant speed considering the news was known in Ameria by morning. Capito too has benefitted from the murder. Capito was part of the delegation of Amerians who came to Sulla to protest. It was Magnus and Capito who informed Chrysogonus at Sulla's camp and Chrysogonus who immediately purchased the property.

Erucius, again, does not escape Cicero's attention. While enumerating his arguments, Cicero attacks him for the weakness of his own when compared to the abundance of facts at Cicero's disposal. Having attacked Magnus with these issues, Cicero repeats them to the jurors, giving him not only a second opportunity to emphasize the good sense of what he is saying, but also to interweave legal objections – Magnus and Capito should not be giving evidence at a trial in which they both have material interests. The attack is comprehensive, compelling and unrelenting. Full of rhetorical flourish, endless questions addressed to Magnus, to Erucius, and to the jurors, presenting a clear counter-argument which is based on motive, outcome and the untrustworthiness and corrupt characters of the individuals involved. Cicero's glee at so comprehensively crushing the prosecution practically flows from the pages.

Attack on Chrysogonus: Sections 124–143

> I come now to a golden name, that of Chrysogonus. For it is under his name that the plot is concealed. How I shall speak about this man, I cannot establish. But nor can I work out how to remain silent.
>
> Cicero, *Pro Sex. Roscio Amerino* 124

Cicero's final attack is against Chrysogonus, Sulla's freedman. Even his name is a gift to Cicero meaning 'golden-born' in Greek (as noted in the extract above) offering the chance to insinuate greed and luxury (distinctly un-Roman virtues) but, that he is caught up in Cicero's accusation of corruption and the purchase of property at a ludicrously low price makes the whole affair a source of delicious opportunity.

Nevertheless, Cicero is very careful to begin with. He makes plain that his attack is one against Chrysogonus, not Sulla, and, much as he does not care about Chrysogonus' feelings, Cicero is aware that others may feel attacked by association. He also looks at the purchase from a distinctly legal standpoint – the paradox of the proscription. If the Elder Roscius was proscribed, unlikely considering his political affiliation, then the auction of his property was legal. But his death and the associated auction took place after the proscription lists were closed, suggesting that an innocent man was killed and his property illegally confiscated. Perhaps, Cicero suggests, he is approaching this in the wrong way but, so he feels, these issues affect us all.

Slowly, however, Cicero turns up the heat. Questions are addressed directly to Chrysogonus (who is almost certainly not present): Why was the property of a good citizen, not an enemy of the state, sold? Why did it take place after the period set out in law? Is Chrysogonus adhering to a stereotype about wicked freedmen who carry out crimes and try to pin responsibility on their former master? Again, Cicero is careful to point out that Sulla has shown his disapproval before and cannot possibly be held accountable because of the vast size of his responsibilities. The climax: a direct accusation against Chrysogonus – *the one architect and contriver of all of this is Chrysogonus alone* (132).

From this, Cicero embarks on an all-out attack on Chrysogonus' penchant for luxury and extravagance, describing in exquisite detail his country houses in southern Italy. The opulence of the image evokes Nero's Golden House or the court of Cleopatra in the mind of a modern reader and is undoubtedly designed to draw on preconceptions of eastern extravagance in the minds of Cicero's audience along with a host of other negative associations. The attack becomes even more personal, criticizing Chrysogonus' appearance and behaviour, focused particularly on the more feminine aspects (strutting around the forum wearing perfume) but climaxing with a distinctly more political tone. Did the nobility struggle to restore the state to stability just so that a freedman could rise to power and be enriched through corruption and theft?

Undoubtedly this is a risky strategy and brings to mind Cicero's opening, drawing attention to the many who could have spoken on behalf of Roscius but chose not to. The repercussions could be serious if misjudged but Cicero plays it well, understanding clearly the limits over which he must not step, the care with which he needs to single out Chrysogonus, the praise which must be shown, the excuses made for Sulla, and, above all, the prejudices and stereotypes which can be put to use most effectively in a Roman courtroom.

Epilogue – the final peroration (**conclusio**): *Sections 143–154 (not in this edition)*

> If he has handed over to you the clothes he wore and the ring from his finger, if, of all his possessions, he has taken nothing beyond his naked body, he begs that you allow him, an innocent man, to live his life supported by his friends in poverty.
>
> Cicero, *Pro Sex. Roscio Amerino* 144

Although these words are addressed to Chrysogonus on Roscius' behalf by Cicero, his aim is not to beg Chrysogonus for mercy. Instead, the *conclusio* is an emotional appeal to the jurors to take pity on Roscius, a man who has lost his father and his home, in the face of an overwhelmingly more powerful man. The focus on Roscius' poverty and the loss that he has experienced is constant, while the mention of what he has remaining (his clothes, his life) serves only to heighten our awareness of the tragedy of Roscius' situation. Entirely reliant on the charity of others, Roscius presents no threat and Cicero urges that he at least be left with his life. The appeal to pity is tempered with warnings, however, a reminder that this case is designed by those who brought it as a tool in their criminality and that, if the jurors do not side with Roscius, they expose themselves to much greater peril in the future.

The outcome

Despite his young age and the power of his opponents, Cicero succeeded in his defence and Roscius was acquitted. Beyond this, little is known for certain. While there is no mention of Chrysogonus in historical records after this time, it is unlikely that Roscius' property was restored to him (indeed, on several occasions throughout the speech Cicero declares that leaving court with his life is enough). Equally unlikely is that any further case was brought against Magnus or Capito. Whether Erucius was subject to judicial proceedings as a false prosecutor is, equally, a mystery.

Reception

> And so, the young man [Roscius], deserted, turned to Cicero. His friends urged him to take the case, since never again would there be such a brilliant and honourable opportunity for fame.
>
> Plutarch, *Cicero* 3.4

When Plutarch introduces *Pro Sex. Roscio Amerino* in his biography of Cicero, he makes clear the opportunity that this presented for Cicero. There is no doubt that the case had public attention and that the individual who defended Roscius successfully would obtain great repute. Cicero himself acknowledges this in his work *Brutus*.

> My first public case, spoken in defence of Sextus Roscius, obtained such great praise that it seemed there was no case for which my advocacy was not best suited.
>
> Cicero, *Brutus* 312

Certainly, therefore, the defence of Roscius was instrumental in establishing Cicero in the public consciousness and a major moment in both his career and his journey to becoming the oratorical giant which he is still recognized as today. Plutarch too notes the fame which Cicero gained, however, he also claims the speech had adverse effects.

> Having taken on the defence, he won the case and attained admiration. But fearing Sulla, he went abroad to Greece, having spread a rumour that his body required attention.
>
> Plutarch, *Cicero* 3.4

In all probability, it is unlikely that Cicero's speech gave Sulla any reason for displeasure. Cicero was extremely careful to discuss the former dictator in only the most diplomatic terms when mentioned in the speech and, perhaps of greater relevance, the purpose of Sulla's new constitution was, in part, to restabilize the Republic. The conduct of Chrysogonus, and others like him, Sulla would have likely considered a threat to his achievements. Plutarch is right, however, that the reason Cicero gave for his departure from Rome was the additional training he required to hone his speech, claiming that his current mode strained his throat and that his doctors had urged him to cease his work in the law courts (Cicero, *Brutus* 314). Nonetheless, Cicero undoubtedly felt pride at his achievement and pleasure at his newfound fame.

> To such great applause did I speak in my youth concerning the punishment of parricide, although after some time I began to feel that it was perhaps too fiery.
>
> Cicero, *On the orator* 107

The fieriness which Cicero criticizes is likely a reflection of the style of speech which he looked to rectify by his travel abroad. In a more general statement concerning his earlier speeches, he suggests the praise he received was not for actual success but for a young man who showed the promise of success (Cicero, *On the orator* 107). Despite Cicero's undoubted youthful exuberance in the delivery of the speech and his own protestations that, at points, the speech is not as polished as others from his later career, there can be no doubt that it is the work of a man committed to the pursuit of justice, who pleads a case with passion, vigour and sincerity. It is for this reason that, as well as being praised by the ancients, it is still considered a work of major importance, admired for the strength of its rhetoric today.

Cicero's style

Beyond the structure of the speech and the force of his arguments, Cicero seeks to strengthen the power of his rhetoric through the precise, regular deployment of specific rhetorical techniques. The exact effect of the techniques which Cicero uses will vary depending on the circumstances, so you should seek to observe them as you read the text and consider how their use enhances his argument at any given time.

The following is a list of techniques to look out for, all taken from the text in this edition with section numbers given in parentheses. It is not exhaustive and there may be others of which you are aware. The list is presented thematically so that techniques can be more easily compared.

Sound of words

alliteration The repetition of consonant sounds: 'quae **t**ot a**c t**ales viros impediat' (5) ('What hinders so many men of such standing') here highlighting the description of *viros*.

assonance The repetition of vowel sounds: '**o**pprimi me **o**nere **o**ffici mal**o** ...' (10) ('I prefer to be crushed by the weight of obligation ...') here highlighting the sacrifice Cicero is willing to make.

Repetition

anaphora The repetition of the same words at the beginning of phrases: '**aut propter** perfidiam ... **aut propter** infirmitatem animi' (10) ('**Either through** treachery **or through** weakness of spirit.') While **aut ... aut ...** is fairly standard, the second pairing with **propter** is not required, adding further weight to the pair of options.

homoioteleuton The deliberate use of words with the same (or similar) grammatical endings: 'perfacile hunc hominem **incautum** et **rusticum** et Romae **ignotum** de medio tolli posse' (20) ('That this man, unsuspecting, rustic and unknown at Rome can be easily done away with.') By ensuring the three adjectives end in the same way, Cicero emphasizes the three qualities.

polyptoton The repetition of different forms of the same word: 'qua vociferatione ... accusatores **uti** consuerunt, ea nos hoc tempore **utimur** …' (12) ('The exclamations which prosecutors usually **use**, we **use** on this occasion…') The repetition of forms of *utor* emphasizes the role reversal.

tautology   The repetition of an idea using different words (saying the same thing twice): 'qui iste **terror** sit et quae tanta **formido** …' (5) ('What that terror and such great fear are …') **terror** and **formido** are essentially the same thing.

Position of words

chiasmus   Position of two ideas in an A-B-B-A format: '<u>causa criminis</u> aut **facti** <u>suspicio</u>' (8) ('a reason for the charge or a suspicion of the deed'). Here the nouns in the nominative are **A** while the genitives which modify these nouns are **B**. The pattern creates a musical quality which emphasizes the ideas.

juxtaposition   The positioning of two ideas side by side in order to highlight their contrasting qualities: 'quo facilius et huius, hominis **innocentissimi, miserias** … cognoscere possitis' ('So that you may understand more easily the miseries of this man, an innocent man.') Where **innocentissimi** and **miserias** are juxtaposed to highlight that an innocent man is suffering.

promotion / delay   The deliberate positioning of words at the beginning or end of sentences or clauses to provide additional emphasis: '**occiditur** ad balneas Pallacinas rediens a cena **Sex. Roscius**' (18) ('Sextus Roscius was killed at the Palatine baths while returning from dinner.') Cicero promotes **occiditur** to emphasize the act while delaying **Sex. Roscius** to create suspense.

Phrasing

antithesis The presentation of contrasting ideas in parallel structures: '**Accusant ei qui** in fortunas huius invaserunt, **causam dicit is, cui** praeter calamitatem nihil reliquerunt ...' (13) ('**They accuse him, men who** have attacked his fortune, **he pleads his case, a man** to whom they have left nothing but disaster ...') Used to illustrate the paradox of the victim having to defend himself against his attackers.

apostrophe Direct address to a named individual: 'Te quoque magno opere, **M. Fanni, quaeso** ...' (11) ('**I entreat you** most sincerely, **Marcus Fannius** ...') Cicero addresses Fannius directly to place the burden of responsibility directly on him.

hendiadys The expression of one idea through two words or phrases: 'mihi **natura pudorque** meus' (9). Literally 'my nature and my modesty', i.e. 'my natural modesty'. This structure places greater emphasis on the individual components.

hyperbole Deliberate exaggeration for the sake of impact: 'ne hic ibidem **ante oculos vestros trucidetur**' (13) ('So that he may not **be slaughtered on the spot before your very eyes**.') Clearly the prosecution had no intention of murdering Roscius during the trial but suggesting it plants the seed and allows the audience to contemplate the other actions they may take.

litotes The use of a negative to emphasize a positive: 'videantur illi **non nihil** tamen in deferendo nomine secuti ...' (8) ('They might appear to have pursued **not nothing** in charging my client ...'), i.e. 'They might appear to have pursued **anything at all** in charging my client ...' emphasizing the extremely low level of Cicero's expectations.

tricolon	The presentation of information in a group of three: 'Nam cum Metellis, Serviliis, Scipionibus erat ei non modo hospitium ...' (15) ('For he had not only ties of friendship with the Metelli, the Servilii, the Scipios ...') This is used here to emphasize the wide range of relationships the elder Roscius had with Rome's great families.
tricolon (crescendo)	The presentation of information in a group of three where the final clause carries greater weight than those preceding: 'cum praesertim nihil esset quod **aut** patri gratius **aut** sibi iucundius **aut re vera** honestius facere posset.' (51) ('Particularly since there was nothing which he was able to do more pleasing to his father, more welcome to himself or, indeed, more honourable.') Here, the sense of country living being honourable is left until the end and strengthened by the inclusion of **re vera**.

Questions

hypophora	The posing of a question which is then immediately answered: 'quibus ... argumentis accusatorem censes uti oportere? Nonne et audaciam ... singularem ostendere' (38) ('Which arguments do you think the accuser ought to use? Surely to show both his outstanding audacity ...') Cicero poses the question in order to demonstrate the tactics which the prosecution ought to have employed.
rhetorical question	A question asked for effect rather than requiring an answer: 'nonne ... hoc indignissimum est vos idoneos habitos ... quod antea ipsi scelere et ferro adsequi consuerunt?' (8) ('Surely this is the most

outrageous thing, that you are considered suitable for those things which they have been accustomed to gain by crime and the sword?') When addressing the jurors in these terms, there can be no doubt that they would consider this outrageous.

Conjunctions

asyndeton A lack of conjunctions which increases pace: 'eam partem causamque **opera, studio, auctoritate** defendit.' (16) ('He defended that faction and cause with **effort, enthusiasm, influence**.') The absence of conjunctions here allows the three ideas to be presented in a way which highlights their complementary nature.

polysyndeton The use of repeated conjunctions to add weight to a phrase: 'quod si **aut** causa criminis **aut** facti suspicio **aut** quaelibet denique vel minima res reperietur ...' (8) ('But if **either** a reason for the charge, **or** suspicion of the deed, **or** finally even the slightest thing is found ...')

Names

(Names given in bold are those usually used to refer to individuals within the text)

Gaius **Erucius**	The advocate for the prosecution. An experienced lawyer but with a dubious family background by Roman standards.
Lucius Cornelius **Chrysogonus**	Freedman of the former dictator, Sulla. Immensely wealthy and powerful at the time of the trial. Implicated in the murder of Sextus Roscius by Cicero, having purchased the estates of the deceased at auction for a vastly reduced price.
Lucius Cornelius **Sulla**	Former general and dictator of Rome, now consul for 80 BC. Powerful and feared, Sulla had instituted wide reaching reforms at Rome and in doing so had killed large numbers of Roman citizens.
Marcus **Fannius**	Praetor for 80 BC and president of the court in which the trial is being heard.
Marcus Tullius **Cicero**	The advocate for the defence undertaking his first criminal trial by making this speech.
Sextus Roscius **the Elder**	The father of Cicero's client. A resident of Ameria murdered on return from a dinner party in Rome late 81 BC.
Sextus Roscius **the Younger**	Cicero's client. The son of the murdered Sextus Roscius now on trial for his father's murder.
Titus Roscius **Capito**	A resident of Ameria and relative of the deceased Sextus Roscius and his son. An associate of Chrysogonus and now in possession of three farms after their purchase. A member of the delegation of Amerians sent to Volaterrae to petition Sulla.
Titus Roscius **Magnus**	A resident of Ameria and relative of the deceased Sextus Roscius and his son. An associate of Chrysogonus and now managing ten farms after their purchase. Magnus is also present in court during the delivery of the speech.

Further reading and resources

There are many works readily available both relating to Cicero and the Late Republic more broadly. The following is a selection which may be of use to A-Level students looking to widen their understanding of the man and the period.

Biographies

Kathryn Tempest's *Cicero: Politics and Persuasion in Ancient Rome* (Bloomsbury Academic, 2013), is an excellent narrative of the life of Cicero arranged chronologically and drawing heavily on Cicero's own writings to create a deep understanding of the man.

Elizabeth Rawson presents a wonderfully rich image of Cicero in her work *Cicero: A Portrait* (Bristol Classical Press, 1994). Arranged by periods of Cicero's life, the work is both detailed and eminently readable.

Arthur Keaveney's *Sulla: The Last Republican* (Routledge, 2005) is a detailed biography of the life of Sulla, the Republican dictator whose achievements and political philosophy shaped the immediate environment in which Cicero delivered the *Pro Sex. Roscio Amerino*.

Study guides

John Murrell's *Cicero and the Roman Republic* (Cambridge University Press, 2008) is a chronological guide to Cicero and the events of his life, based entirely on ancient source material. A great way of getting a first-hand look at the period through the eyes of the ancients.

Fiction

Robert Harris' *Cicero* trilogy of historical novels (*Imperium*, *Lustrum*, *Dictator*, Hutchinson, 2021) is an excellent way of getting to know both Cicero and the major events of the Late Republic, written in a style which is both accessible and enormously engaging.

Histories of the Late Republic

Tom Holland's best-selling *Rubicon: the triumph and tragedy of the Roman Republic* (Abacus, 2004) is an extremely useful introduction to the period written straightforwardly and entertainingly with sufficient depth to gain a good understanding of events and key individuals.

David M. Gwynn's *The Roman Republic: A Very Short Introduction* (Oxford University Press, 2012) is, as the name would suggest, a great way of getting a quick overview of the Republic from its foundations to its fall.

Translations

Michael Grant's translation of *Pro Sex. Roscio Amerino* in the Penguin Classics *Cicero: Murder Trials* (Penguin Books, revised 1990) is very readable but sticks close enough to the Latin to retain much of the flavour of Cicero's original rendering.

Series and documentaries

Timewatch's *Murder in Rome* (2005 starring Paul Rhys as Cicero and Owen Teale as Erucius) is a short documentary produced for the BBC featuring a dramatization of the *Pro Roscio* and is a great way of getting a more visual understanding of the experience of a Roman courtroom.

HBO's gritty, violent (and at times explicit) drama, *Rome* (2005-7) interweaves fictional characters and storylines with historical characters and events, following the life of Julius Caesar and the fall of the Roman Republic and culminating with the rise of Augustus.

Text

1–5: Cicero opens the speech by concentrating on his own inexperience in the lawcourts but his desire to give Sextus Roscius some kind of defence.

5. forsitan quaeratis, qui iste terror sit et quae tanta formido, quae tot ac tales viros impediat quo minus pro capite et fortunis alterius, quem ad modum consuerunt, causam velint dicere. quod adhuc vos ignorare non mirum est, propterea quod consulto ab accusatoribus eius rei, quae conflavit hoc iudicium, mentio facta non est.

6. quae res ea est? bona patris huiusce Sex. Roscii, quae sunt sexagiens, quae de viro fortissimo et clarissimo L. Sulla, quem honoris causa nomino, duobus milibus nummum sese dicit emisse adulescens vel potentissimus hoc tempore nostrae civitatis, L. Cornelius Chrysogonus. is a vobis, iudices, hoc postulat, ut, quoniam in alienam pecuniam tam plenam atque praeclaram nullo iure invaserit, quoniamque ei pecuniae vita Sex. Roscii obstare atque officere videatur, deleatis ex animo suo suspicionem omnem metumque tollatis: sese hoc incolumi non arbitratur huius innocentis patrimonium tam amplum et copiosum posse obtinere, damnato et eiecto sperat se posse, quod adeptus est per scelus, id per luxuriam effundere atque consumere. hunc sibi ex animo scrupulum, qui se dies noctesque stimulat ac pungit, ut evellatis, postulat, ut ad hanc suam praedam tam nefariam adiutores vos profiteamini.

7. si vobis aequa et honesta postulatio videtur, iudices, ego contra brevem postulationem adfero et, quo modo mihi persuadeo, aliquanto aequiorem. primum a Chrysogono peto ut pecunia fortunisque nostris contentus sit, sanguinem et vitam ne petat; deinde a vobis, iudices, ut audacium sceleri resistatis, innocentium calamitatem levetis et in causa Sex. Roscii periculum, quod in omnes intenditur, propulsetis.

8. quod si aut causa criminis aut facti suspicio aut quaelibet denique vel minima res reperietur, quam ob rem videantur illi non nihil tamen in deferendo nomine secuti, postremo si praeter eam praedam, quam dixi, quicquam aliud causae inveneritis, non recusamus, quin illorum libidini Sex. Rosci vita dedatur. sin aliud agitur nihil nisi, ut eis ne quid desit, quibus satis nihil est, si hoc solum hoc tempore pugnatur, ut ad illam opimam praeclaramque praedam damnatio Sex. Rosci velut cumulus accedat, nonne cum multa indigna tum vel hoc indignissimum est vos idoneos habitos, per quorum sententias iusque iurandum id adsequantur, quod antea ipsi scelere et ferro adsequi consuerunt? qui ex civitate in senatum propter dignitatem, ex senatu in hoc consilium delecti estis propter severitatem, ab his hoc postulare homines sicarios atque gladiatores, non modo ut supplicia vitent, quae a vobis pro maleficiis suis metuere atque horrere debent, verum etiam ut spoliis ex hoc iudicio ornati auctique discedant?

9. his de rebus tantis tamque atrocibus neque satis me commode dicere neque satis graviter conqueri neque satis libere vociferari posse intellego. nam commoditati ingenium, gravitati aetas, libertati tempora sunt impedimento. huc accedit summus timor, quem mihi natura pudorque meus attribuit, et vestra dignitas et vis adversariorum et Sex. Rosci pericula. quapropter vos oro atque obsecro, iudices, ut attente bonaque cum venia verba mea audiatis.

10. fide sapientiaque vestra fretus plus oneris sustuli quam ferre me posse intellego. hoc onus si vos aliqua ex parte adlevabitis, feram ut potero studio et industria, iudices; sin a vobis, id quod non spero, deserar, tamen animo non deficiam et id quod suscepi, quoad potero perferam. quod si perferre non potero, opprimi me onere offici malo quam id, quod mihi cum fide semel impositum est, aut propter perfidiam abicere aut propter infirmitatem animi deponere.

11. te quoque magno opere, M. Fanni, quaeso, ut, qualem te iam antea populo Romano praebuisti, cum huic eidem quaestioni iudex praeesses, talem te et nobis et rei publicae hoc tempore impertias. quanta multitudo hominum convenerit ad hoc iudicium, vides; quae sit omnium mortalium exspectatio, quae cupiditas, ut acria ac severa iudicia fiant, intellegis. longo intervallo iudicium inter sicarios hoc primum committitur, cum interea caedes indignissimae maximaeque factae sunt; omnes hanc quaestionem te praetore manifestis maleficiis cotidianoque sanguine dignissimam sperant futuram.

12. qua vociferatione in ceteris iudiciis accusatores uti consuerunt, ea nos hoc tempore utimur qui causam dicimus. petimus abs te, M. Fanni, a vobisque, iudices, ut quam acerrime maleficia vindicetis, ut quam fortissime hominibus audacissimis resistatis, ut hoc cogitetis, nisi in hac causa, qui vester animus sit, ostendetis, eo prorumpere hominum cupiditatem et scelus et audaciam, ut non modo clam, verum etiam hic in foro ante tribunal tuum, M. Fanni, ante pedes vestros, iudices, inter ipsa subsellia caedes futurae sint.

13. etenim quid aliud hoc iudicio temptatur nisi, ut id fieri liceat? accusant ei qui in fortunas huius invaserunt, causam dicit is, cui praeter calamitatem nihil reliquerunt; accusant ei, quibus occidi patrem Sex. Rosci bono fuit, causam dicit is, cui non modo luctum mors patris attulit, verum etiam egestatem; accusant ei, qui hunc ipsum iugulare summe cupierunt, causam dicit is, qui etiam ad hoc ipsum iudicium cum praesidio venit, ne hic ibidem ante oculos vestros trucidetur; denique accusant ei, quos populus poscit, causam dicit is, qui unus relictus ex illorum nefaria caede restat.

14. atque ut facilius intellegere possitis, iudices, ea quae facta sunt indigniora esse, quam haec sunt quae dicimus, ab initio res quem ad modum gesta sit vobis exponemus, quo facilius et huius, hominis innocentissimi, miserias et illorum audacias cognoscere possitis et rei publicae calamitatem.

15. Sex. Roscius, pater huiusce, municeps Amerinus fuit, cum genere et nobilitate et pecunia non modo sui municipi, verum etiam eius vicinitatis facile primus, tum gratia atque hospitiis florens hominum nobilissimorum. nam cum Metellis, Serviliis, Scipionibus erat ei non modo hospitium, verum etiam domesticus usus et consuetudo, quas, ut aequum est, familias honestatis amplitudinisque gratia nomino. itaque ex suis omnibus commodis hoc solum filio reliquit; nam patrimonium domestici praedones vi ereptum possident, fama et vita innocentis ab hospitibus amicisque paternis defenditur.

16. hic cum omni tempore nobilitatis fautor fuisset, tum hoc tumultu proximo, cum omnium nobilium dignitas et salus in discrimen veniret, praeter ceteros in ea vicinitate eam partem causamque opera, studio, auctoritate defendit. etenim rectum putabat pro eorum honestate se pugnare, propter quos ipse honestissimus inter suos numerabatur. postea quam victoria constituta est ab armisque recessimus, cum proscriberentur homines atque ex omni regione caperentur ei, qui adversarii fuisse putabantur, erat ille Romae frequens atque in foro et in ore omnium cotidie versabatur, magis ut exsultare victoria nobilitatis videretur quam timere, ne quid ex ea calamitatis sibi accideret.

17. erant ei veteres inimicitiae cum duobus Rosciis Amerinis, quorum alterum sedere in accusatorum subselliis video, alterum tria huiusce praedia possidere audio; quas inimicitias si tam cavere potuisset, quam metuere solebat, viveret. neque enim, iudices, iniuria metuebat. nam duo isti sunt T. Roscii, quorum alteri Capitoni cognomen est, iste, qui adest, Magnus vocatur, homines eius modi: alter plurimarum palmarum vetus ac nobilis gladiator habetur, hic autem nuper se ad eum lanistam contulit, quique ante hanc pugnam tiro esset quod sciam, facile ipsum magistrum scelere audaciaque superavit.

18. nam cum hic Sex. Roscius esset Ameriae, T. autem iste Roscius Romae, cum hic filius adsiduus in praediis esset cumque se voluntate patris rei familiari vitaeque rusticae dedisset, iste autem frequens Romae esset, occiditur ad balneas Pallacinas rediens a cena Sex. Roscius. spero ex hoc ipso non esse obscurum, ad quem suspicio malefici pertineat; verum id, quod adhuc est suspiciosum, nisi perspicuum res ipsa fecerit, hunc adfinem culpae iudicatote.

19. occiso Sex. Roscio primus Ameriam nuntiat Mallius Glaucia quidam, homo tenuis, libertinus, cliens et familiaris istius T. Rosci, et nuntiat domum non fili, sed T. Capitonis inimici; et cum post horam primam noctis occisus esset, primo diluculo nuntius hic Ameriam venit; decem horis nocturnis sex et quinquaginta milia passuum cisiis pervolavit, non modo ut exoptatum inimico nuntium primus adferret, sed etiam cruorem inimici quam recentissimum telumque paulo ante e corpore extractum ostenderet.

20. quadriduo quo haec gesta sunt res ad Chrysogonum in castra L. Sullae Volaterras defertur; magnitudo pecuniae demonstratur; bonitas praediorum – nam fundos decem et tris reliquit, qui Tiberim fere omnes tangunt – huius inopia et solitudo commemoratur; demonstrant, cum pater huiusce Sex. Roscius, homo tam splendidus et gratiosus, nullo negotio sit occisus, perfacile hunc hominem incautum et rusticum et Romae ignotum de medio tolli posse; ad eam rem operam suam pollicentur.

21. ne diutius teneam, iudices, societas coitur. cum nulla iam proscriptionis mentio fieret, cum etiam, qui antea metuerant, redirent ac iam defunctos sese periculis arbitrarentur, nomen refertur in tabulas Sex. Rosci, hominis studiosissimi nobilitatis; manceps fit Chrysogonus; tria praedia vel nobilissima Capitoni propria traduntur, quae hodie possidet; in reliquas omnes fortunas iste T. Roscius nomine Chrysogoni, quem ad modum ipse dicit, impetum facit. haec omnia, iudices, imprudente L. Sulla facta esse certo scio.

22. neque enim mirum, cum eodem tempore et ea, quae praeterita sunt, reparet et ea, quae videntur instare, praeparet, cum et pacis constituendae rationem et belli gerendi potestatem solus habeat, cum omnes in unum spectent, unus omnia gubernet, cum tot tantisque negotiis distentus sit, ut respirare libere non possit, si aliquid non animadvertat, cum praesertim tam multi occupationem eius observent tempusque aucupentur ut, simul atque ille despexerit, aliquid huiusce modi moliantur. huc accedit quod, quamvis ille felix sit, sicut est, tamen in tanta felicitate nemo potest esse in magna familia, qui neminem neque servum neque libertum improbum habeat.

23. interea iste T. Roscius, vir optimus, procurator Chrysogoni, Ameriam venit, in praedia huius invadit, hunc miserum, luctu perditum, qui nondum etiam omnia paterno funeri iusta solvisset, nudum eicit domo atque focis patriis disque penatibus praecipitem, iudices, exturbat, ipse amplissimae pecuniae fit dominus. qui in sua re fuisset egentissimus, erat, ut fit, insolens in aliena; multa palam domum suam auferebat; plura clam de medio removebat, non pauca suis adiutoribus large effuseque donabat, reliqua constituta auctione vendebat.

24. quod Amerinis usque eo visum est indignum, ut urbe tota fletus gemitusque fieret. etenim multa simul ante oculos versabantur, mors hominis florentissimi, Sex. Rosci, crudelissima, fili autem eius egestas indignissima, cui de tanto patrimonio praedo iste nefarius ne iter quidem ad sepulcrum patrium reliquisset, bonorum emptio flagitiosa, possessio, furta, rapinae, donationes. nemo erat, qui non audere omnia mallet quam videre in Sex. Rosci, viri optimi atque honestissimi, bonis iactantem se ac dominantem T. Roscium.

25. itaque decurionum decretum statim fit, ut decem primi proficiscantur ad L. Sullam doceantque eum, qui vir Sex. Roscius fuerit, conquerantur de istorum scelere et iniuriis, orent, ut et illius mortui famam et fili innocentis fortunas conservatas velit. atque ipsum decretum, quaeso, cognoscite.

[decretum decurionum.]

legati in castra veniunt. intellegitur, iudices, id quod iam ante dixi, imprudente L. Sulla scelera haec et flagitia fieri. nam statim Chrysogonus et ipse ad eos accedit et homines nobilis adlegat, qui peterent, ne ad Sullam adirent, et omnia Chrysogonum, quae vellent, esse facturum pollicerentur.

26. usque adeo autem ille pertimuerat, ut mori mallet, quam de his rebus Sullam doceri. homines antiqui, qui ex sua natura ceteros fingerent, cum ille confirmaret sese nomen Sex. Rosci de tabulis exempturum, praedia vacua filio traditurum, cumque id ita futurum T. Roscius Capito, qui in decem legatis erat, appromitteret, crediderunt; Ameriam re inorata reverterunt. ac primo rem differre cotidie ac procrastinare isti coeperunt, deinde aliquanto lentius nihil agere atque deludere, postremo, id quod facile intellectum est, insidias vitae huiusce

Sex. Rosci parare neque sese arbitrari posse diutius alienam pecuniam domino incolumi obtinere.

27. quod hic simul atque sensit, de amicorum cognatorumque sententia Romam confugit et sese ad Caeciliam, Nepotis sororem, Baliarici filiam, quam honoris causa nomino, contulit, qua pater usus erat plurimum; in qua muliere, iudices, etiam nunc, id quod omnes semper existimaverunt, quasi exempli causa vestigia antiqui offici remanent. ea Sex. Roscium inopem, eiectum domo atque expulsum ex suis bonis, fugientem latronum tela et minas recepit domum hospitique oppresso iam desperatoque ab omnibus opitulata est. eius virtute, fide, diligentia factum est, ut hic potius vivus in reos quam occisus in proscriptos referretur.

28. nam postquam isti intellexerunt summa diligentia vitam Sex. Rosci custodiri neque sibi ullam caedis faciendae potestatem dari, consilium ceperunt plenum sceleris et audaciae, ut nomen huius de parricidio deferrent, ut ad eam rem aliquem accusatorem veterem compararent, qui de ea re posset dicere aliquid, in qua re nulla subesset suspicio, denique ut, quoniam crimine non poterant, tempore ipso pugnarent. ita loqui homines: quod iudicia tam diu facta non essent, condemnari eum oportere, qui primus in iudicium adductus esset; huic autem patronos propter Chrysogoni gratiam defuturos; de bonorum venditione et de ista societate verbum esse facturum neminem; ipso nomine parricidi et atrocitate criminis fore, ut hic nullo negotio tolleretur, cum ab nullo defensus esset.

29. hoc consilio atque adeo hac amentia impulsi, quem ipsi, cum cuperent, non potuerunt occidere, eum iugulandum vobis tradiderunt.

29. quid primum querar aut unde potissimum, iudices, ordiar aut quod aut a quibus auxilium petam? deorumne immortalium, populine Romani, vestramne, qui summam potestatem habetis, hoc tempore fidem implorem?

30. pater occisus nefarie, domus obsessa ab inimicis, bona adempta, possessa, direpta, fili vita infesta, saepe ferro atque insidiis appetita. quid ab his tot maleficiis sceleris abesse videtur? tamen haec aliis nefariis cumulant atque adaugent, crimen incredibile confingunt, testes in hunc et accusatores huiusce pecunia comparant; hanc condicionem misero ferunt, ut optet, utrum malit cervices T. Roscio dare an insutus in culleum per summum dedecus vitam amittere. patronos huic defuturos putaverunt; desunt; qui libere dicat, qui cum fide defendat, id quod in hac causa satis est, non deest profecto, iudices.

31. et forsitan in suscipienda causa temere impulsus adulescentia fecerim; quoniam quidem semel suscepi, licet, hercules, undique omnes minae, terrores periculaque impendeant omnia, succurram ac subibo. certum est deliberatumque, quae ad causam pertinere arbitror, omnia non modo dicere, verum etiam libenter, audacter libereque dicere; nulla res tanta exsistet, iudices, ut possit vim mihi maiorem adhibere metus quam fides.

32. etenim quis tam dissoluto animo est, qui, haec cum videat, tacere ac neglegere possit? patrem meum, cum proscriptus non esset, iugulastis, occisum in proscriptorum numerum rettulistis, me domo mea per vim expulistis, patrimonium meum possidetis. quid voltis amplius? etiamne ad subsellia cum ferro atque telis venistis, ut hic aut iuguletis aut condemnetis?

33–36: Cicero considers the use of the law courts as a weapon by those wishing to remove their enemies. In Section 35 Cicero begins his partitio.

37. occidisse patrem Sex. Roscius arguitur. scelestum, di immortales, ac nefarium facinus atque eius modi, quo uno maleficio scelera omnia complexa esse videantur! etenim si, id quod praeclare a sapientibus dicitur, voltu saepe laeditur pietas, quod supplicium satis acre reperietur in eum, qui mortem obtulerit parenti? pro quo mori ipsum, si res postularet, iura divina atque humana cogebant.

38. in hoc tanto, tam atroci, tam singulari maleficio, quod ita raro exstitit, ut, si quando auditum sit, portenti ac prodigi simile numeretur, quibus tandem tu, C. Eruci, argumentis accusatorem censes uti oportere? nonne et audaciam eius, qui in crimen vocetur, singularem ostendere et mores feros immanemque naturam et vitam vitiis flagitiisque omnibus deditam, et denique omnia ad perniciem profligata atque perdita? quorum tu nihil in Sex. Roscium ne obiciendi quidem causa contulisti.

39. patrem occidit Sex. Roscius. qui homo? adulescentulus corruptus et ab hominibus nequam inductus? annos natus maior quadraginta. vetus videlicet sicarius, homo audax et saepe in caede versatus. at hoc ab accusatore ne dici quidem audistis. luxuries igitur hominem nimirum et aeris alieni magnitudo et indomitae animi cupiditates ad hoc scelus impulerunt. de luxuria purgavit Erucius, cum dixit hunc ne in convivio quidem ullo fere interfuisse. nihil autem umquam debuit. cupiditates porro quae possunt esse in eo, qui, ut ipse accusator obiecit, ruri semper habitarit et in agro colendo vixerit? quae vita maxime disiuncta a cupiditate et cum officio coniuncta est.

40. quae res igitur tantum istum furorem Sex. Roscio obiecit? 'patri' inquit 'non placebat.' patri non placebat? quam ob causam? necesse est enim eam quoque iustam et magnam et perspicuam fuisse. nam ut illud incredibile est, mortem oblatam esse patri a filio sine plurimis et maximis causis, sic hoc veri simile non est, odio fuisse parenti filium sine causis multis et magnis et necessariis.

41. rursus igitur eodem revertamur et quaeramus, quae tanta vitia fuerint in unico filio, qua re is patri displiceret. at perspicuum est nullum fuisse. pater igitur amens, qui odisset eum sine causa quem procrearat? at is quidem fuit omnium constantissimus. Ergo illud iam perspicuum profecto est, si neque amens pater neque perditus filius fuerit, neque odi causam patri neque sceleris filio fuisse.

42. 'nescio' inquit 'quae causa odi fuerit; fuisse odium intellego quia antea, cum duos filios haberet, illum alterum qui mortuus est secum omni tempore volebat esse, hunc in praedia rustica relegarat.' quod Erucio accidebat in mala nugatoriaque accusatione, idem mihi usu venit in causa optima. ille quo modo crimen commenticium confirmaret non inveniebat, ego res tam leves qua ratione infirmem ac diluam reperire non possum.

43. quid ais, Eruci? tot praedia tam pulchra, tam fructuosa Sex. Roscius filio suo relegationis ac supplici gratia colenda ac tuenda tradiderat? quid? hoc patres familiae qui liberos habent, praesertim homines illius ordinis ex municipiis rusticanis, nonne optatissimum sibi putant esse filios suos rei familiari maxime servire et in praediis colendis operae plurimum studique consumere?

44. an amandarat hunc sic ut esset in agro ac tantum modo aleretur ad villam, ut commodis omnibus careret? quid? si constat hunc non modo colendis praediis praefuisse sed certis fundis patre vivo frui solitum esse, tamenne haec a te vita eius rusticana relegatio atque amandatio appellabitur? vides, Eruci, quantum distet argumentatio tua ab re ipsa atque a veritate. quod consuetudine patres faciunt, id quasi novum reprehendis; quod benevolentia fit, id odio factum criminaris; quod honoris causa pater filio suo concessit, id eum supplici causa fecisse dicis.

45. neque haec tu non intellegis, sed usque eo quid arguas non habes, ut non modo tibi contra nos dicendum putes verum etiam contra rerum naturam contraque consuetudinem hominum contraque opiniones omnium.

at enim, cum duos filios haberet, alterum a se non dimittebat, alterum ruri esse patiebatur. quaeso, Eruci, ut hoc in bonam partem accipias; non enim exprobrandi causa sed commonendi gratia dicam.

46. si tibi fortuna non dedit, ut patre certo nascerere, ex quo intellegere posses, qui animus patrius in liberos esset, at natura certe dedit, ut humanitatis non parum haberes; eo accessit studium doctrinae, ut ne a litteris quidem alienus esses. ecquid tandem tibi videtur, ut ad fabulas veniamus, senex ille Caecilianus minoris facere Eutychum, filium rusticum, quam illum alterum, Chaerestratum? – nam, ut opinor, hoc nomine est – alterum in urbe secum honoris causa habere, alterum rus supplici causa relegasse?

47. 'quid ad istas ineptias abis?' inquies. quasi vero mihi difficile sit quamvis multos nominatim proferre, ne longius abeam, vel tribules vel vicinos meos qui suos liberos quos plurimi faciunt agricolas adsiduos esse cupiunt. verum homines notos sumere odiosum est, cum et illud incertum sit velintne ei sese nominari, et nemo vobis magis notus futurus sit quam est hic Eutychus, et certe ad rem nihil intersit utrum hunc ego comicum adulescentem an aliquem ex agro Veienti nominem. etenim haec conficta arbitror esse a poetis ut effictos nostros mores in alienis personis expressamque imaginem vitae cotidianae videremus.

48. age nunc, refer animum sis ad veritatem et considera non modo in Umbria atque in ea vicinitate sed in his veteribus municipiis quae studia a patribus familias maxime laudentur; iam profecto te intelleges inopia criminum summam laudem Sex. Roscio vitio et culpae dedisse. ac non modo hoc patrum voluntate liberi faciunt sed permultos et ego novi et, nisi me fallit animus, unus quisque vestrum qui et ipsi incensi sunt studio quod ad agrum colendum attinet, vitamque hanc rusticam, quam tu probro et crimini putas esse oportere, et honestissimam et suavissimam esse arbitrantur.

49. quid censes hunc ipsum Sex. Roscium quo studio et qua intellegentia esse in rusticis rebus? ut ex his propinquis eius, hominibus honestissimis, audio, non tu in isto artificio accusatorio callidior es quam hic in suo. verum, ut opinor, quoniam ita Chrysogono videtur qui huic nullum praedium reliquit, et artificium obliviscatur et studium deponat licebit. quod tametsi miserum et indignum est, feret tamen aequo animo, iudices, si per vos vitam et famam potest obtinere; hoc vero est quod ferri non potest, si et in hanc calamitatem venit propter praediorum bonitatem et multitudinem et quod ea studiose coluit, id erit ei maxime fraudi, ut parum miseriae sit quod aliis coluit non sibi, nisi etiam quod omnino coluit crimini fuerit.

50. ne tu, Eruci, accusator esses ridiculus, si illis temporibus natus esses cum ab aratro arcessebantur qui consules fierent. etenim qui praeesse agro colendo flagitium putes, profecto illum Atilium quem sua manu spargentem semen qui missi erant convenerunt hominem turpissimum atque inhonestissimum iudicares. at hercule maiores nostri longe aliter et de illo et de ceteris talibus viris existimabant itaque ex minima tenuissimaque re publica maximam et florentissimam nobis reliquerunt. suos enim agros studiose colebant, non alienos cupide appetebant; quibus rebus et agris et urbibus et nationibus rem publicam atque hoc imperium et populi Romani nomen auxerunt.

51. neque ego haec eo profero quo conferenda sint cum hisce de quibus nunc quaerimus, sed ut illud intellegatur, cum apud maiores nostros summi viri clarissimique homines qui omni tempore ad gubernacula rei publicae sedere debebant tamen in agris quoque colendis aliquantum operae temporisque consumpserint, ignosci oportere ei homini qui se fateatur esse rusticum, cum ruri adsiduus semper vixerit, cum praesertim nihil esset quod aut patri gratius aut sibi iucundius aut re vera honestius facere posset.

52. odium igitur acerrimum patris in filium ex hoc, opinor, ostenditur, Eruci, quod hunc ruri esse patiebatur. numquid est aliud? 'immo vero' inquit 'est; nam istum exheredare in animo habebat.' audio; nunc dicis aliquid quod ad rem pertineat; nam illa, opinor, tu quoque concedis levia esse atque inepta: 'convivia cum patre non inibat.' quippe, qui ne in oppidum quidem nisi perraro veniret. 'domum suam istum non fere quisquam vocabat.' nec mirum, qui neque in urbe viveret neque revocaturus esset.

53. verum haec tu quoque intellegis esse nugatoria; illud quod coepimus videamus, quo certius argumentum odi reperiri nullo modo potest. 'exheredare pater filium cogitabat.' mitto quaerere qua de causa; quaero qui scias; tametsi te dicere atque enumerare causas omnis oportebat, et id erat certi accusatoris officium qui tanti sceleris argueret explicare omnia vitia ac peccata fili quibus incensus parens potuerit animum inducere ut naturam ipsam vinceret, ut amorem illum penitus insitum eiceret ex animo, ut denique patrem esse sese obliviscereretur; quae sine magnis huiusce peccatis accidere potuisse non arbitror.

54. verum concedo tibi ut ea praetereas quae, cum taces, nulla esse concedis; illud quidem, voluisse exheredare, certe tu planum facere debes. quid ergo adfers qua re id factum putemus? vere nihil potes dicere; finge aliquid saltem commode ut ne plane videaris id facere quod aperte facis, huius miseri fortunis et horum virorum talium dignitati inludere. exheredare filium voluit. quam ob causam? 'nescio.' exheredavitne? 'non.' quis prohibuit? 'cogitabat.' cogitabat? cui dixit? 'nemini.' quid est aliud iudicio ac legibus ac maiestate vestra abuti ad quaestum atque ad libidinem nisi hoc modo accusare atque id obicere quod planum facere non modo non possis verum ne coneris quidem?

55. nemo nostrum est, Eruci, quin sciat tibi inimicitias cum Sex. Roscio nullas esse; vident omnes qua de causa huic inimicus venias; sciunt huiusce pecuniam te adductum esse. quid ergo est? ita tamen quaestus te cupidum esse oportebat ut horum existimationem et legem Remmiam putares aliquid valere oportere.

56. accusatores multos esse in civitate utile est, ut metu contineatur audacia; verum tamen hoc ita est utile, ut ne plane inludamur ab accusatoribus. Innocens est quispiam, verum tamen, quamquam abest a culpa, suspicione tamen non caret; tametsi miserum est, tamen ei, qui hunc accuset, possim aliquo modo ignoscere. cum enim aliquid habeat, quod possit criminose ac suspiciose dicere, aperte ludificari et calumniari sciens non videatur. qua re facile omnes patimur esse quam plurimos accusatores, quod innocens, si accusatus sit, absolvi potest, nocens, nisi accusatus fuerit, condemnari non potest; utilius est autem absolvi innocentem quam nocentem causam non dicere. anseribus cibaria publice locantur et canes aluntur in Capitolio, ut significent si fures venerint. at fures internoscere non possunt, significant tamen, si qui noctu in Capitolium venerint et quia id est suspiciosum, tametsi bestiae sunt, tamen in eam partem potius peccant quae est cautior. quod si luce quoque canes latrent, cum deos salutatum aliqui venerint, opinor, eis crura suffringantur, quod acres sint etiam tum, cum suspicio nulla sit.

57. simillima est accusatorum ratio. alii vestrum anseres sunt, qui tantum modo clamant, nocere non possunt, alii canes, qui et latrare et mordere possunt. cibaria vobis praeberi videmus; vos autem maxime debetis in eos impetum facere, qui merentur. hoc populo gratissimum est. deinde, si voletis, etiam tum cum verisimile erit aliquem commisisse, in suspicione latratote; id quoque concedi potest. sin autem sic agetis ut arguatis aliquem patrem occidisse neque dicere possitis aut qua re aut quo modo, ac tantum modo sine suspicione latrabitis, crura quidem vobis nemo suffringet, sed, si ego hos bene novi, litteram illam cui vos usque eo inimici estis ut etiam Kal. omnis oderitis ita vehementer ad caput adfigent ut postea neminem alium nisi fortunas vestras accusare possitis.

58–154: For a summary of the rest of the speech, see Introduction pp.15–23.

Commentary Notes

1–5: Cicero opens the speech by suggesting that the jurors will be amazed that it is he who has stood up to defend Sextus Roscius rather than any of the more distinguished persons present. They are here, he says, so that they can be seen to fulfil their duty in the face of an unjust charge but they cannot speak openly as this would put them in danger. Cicero, on the other hand, is not any bolder or keener than the others but has considerably less public fame. As a man just entering public life, his words, he suggests, will be taken less seriously and will not travel as far as similar words spoken by a more well-known orator. Furthermore, well-established orators may have felt more at liberty to refuse a case but, as a young man being helped on his way, Cicero did not feel capable of denying the request to defend Sextus Roscius when it came from such eminent and influential individuals.

More than this, however, Cicero asserts that, since he can speak with the least risk to himself, he chose to defend Sextus Roscius so that, far from providing Roscius with the best defence available, Roscius might at least have someone speaking on his behalf.

5

forsitan quaeratis: **forsitan** is usually found with the subjunctive in Republican literature – *perhaps you might ask*.... Cicero frequently engages in this technique (*hypophora*) where he answers a question he imagines another party (in this case the jury) to have asked. In doing so, it allows him to appear to be engaging in dialogue while still controlling the terms of the argument. The answer to the question will come in Section 6.

qui iste terror: both **qui** and **iste** modify **terror** which follows – *what is that fear ...?* **quae tanta formido** works in the same fashion. In the opening of the speech, Cicero has suggested that fear means he is the only one willing to defend Sextus Roscius. The use of both terms (*tautology*) adds additional emphasis to his words.

tot ac tales viros: Cicero refers again to the eminent orators present in the courtroom whom one might have expected to be defending Sextus Roscius in his place. The alliteration (**t**ot ac **t**ales) and use of hendiadys (*so many and such men = so many men of this type*) stresses how many individuals of greater experience are present.

impediat quo minus: *impedio* is found with a variety of structures including with *ne*, *quin* and *quominus* (or, as in this case, **quo minus** as two separate words). Literally *hinders them by which less they might ...* consider *hinders them from* or *prevents them from*.

pro capite: here *life* – Roscius is being tried on a capital charge and will be executed if found guilty (see Introduction).

et fortunis: although in a sense a tautology (Roscius' life and fate are bound together), *fortuna* is often paired with *caput* in these instances as Roscius' guilt would have resulted in the confiscation of his property as well as his execution.

causam ... dicere: as a phrase – *to plead a case*.

quod: connecting relative – *[that you are ignorant of] this ...*, i.e. what the terror is which holds back other speakers.

propterea quod: as a phrase – *on account of the fact that*. . . .

mentio facta non est: **mentio** is the subject within this clause (*mention has not been made*. . .) but Cicero delays the phrase until the end of the sentence to maximize impact. Surely the jurors know what has caused this case? Not in Cicero's opinion and he is only too willing to enlighten them. **eius rei** modifies **mentio** – *no mention of that business [which]*. . . .

6

quae res: i.e. the matter which the prosecution has failed to mention.

bona patris huiusce Sex. Roscii: here the neuter plural **bona** stands for the elder Roscius' possessions. **huiusce** is an emphatic form of *huius* which agrees with **Sex. Roscii** in the genitive – *of this man, Sextus Roscius*. **Sex.** is a standard abbreviation for the name Sextus. Sextus Roscius here refers to the defendant in this case rather than his father.

quae sunt sexagiens: *which are valued at six million sestertii / which amount to six million sestertii*.

quae . . . sese dicit emisse adulescens . . . L. Cornelius Chrysogonus: the structure may seem complex here as Cicero has deliberately left the subject until the end (see below) while the use of **quae** has changed, becoming the object. A more straightforward structure might be:

- **quae** – *which*
- **adulescens L. Cornelius Chrysogonus dicit** – *the youth Lucius Cornelius Chrysogonus says*
- **sese emisse** – *he bought*
- **de L. Sulla** – *from Lucius Sulla*.

Remember, however, that Cicero has chosen this phrasing deliberately and it may be beneficial to reflect this when translating. Remember too that Chrysogonus' purchase of property would have been from a state auction, not directly from Sulla but, by putting these words into Chrysogonus' mouth, Cicero states clearly who authorized the purchase.

L. Sulla: Lucius Sulla (**L.** is a standard abbreviation), dictator of Rome who has recently resigned office. The mention of his name so early in the speech gives the case an immediate political dimension. Cicero is extremely careful to speak in favourable terms about Sulla whenever he is mentioned (for instance describing him as **fortissimo et clarissimo**) to ensure that he cannot be accused of badmouthing so powerful a politician. While it is possible that his complimentary tone when referencing Sulla may not be entirely sincere, his attack is clearly directed at Sulla's freedman Chrysogonus, not Sulla himself.

duobus milibus nummum: *two thousand sestertii* – the contrast is stark: no man should have been able to purchase such extensive property (even property confiscated by the state) at such a knock-down price. For context, property of 800,000 sestertii was the qualification for entry to the senate at this time (a fortune which some senators in the Late Republic struggled to maintain). For Chrysogonus to purchase property many times that value at such a small fraction of the cost immediately implies suspicious activity on his part.

adulescens vel potentissimus: the use of the term **adulescens** is negative, looking to diminish Chrysogonus (whom it describes) suggesting inexperience and impetuousness. **vel** should be taken as *perhaps*.

L. Cornelius Chrysogonus: A freedman of the former dictator, Sulla, Lucius Cornelius Chrysogonus had amassed considerable wealth and influence through his association with his powerful former master. His name is in part that of Sulla as it was customary for freedmen to take their master's name at the point they were freed. The name Chrysogonus is also something of a gift for Cicero being taken from the Greek χρυσόγονος (*chrusogonos*) meaning *born of gold*, instantly giving Chrysogonus a more ostentatious and untrustworthy eastern flavour and distancing him from idealized Roman values. Cicero places his name at the end as a climax which, despite speaking for the defence, signals his willingness to accuse.

is a vobis ... hoc postulat: Cicero is a master of taking a case and turning it into something considerably bigger than it might seem. Cicero does not believe this case is about whether Roscius killed his father but rather whether a freedman who has become so excessively powerful can use the legal system to eliminate an individual who poses a threat to him and legitimize his illegal theft of property. That Cicero phrases this as a request (**hoc postulat**) from Chrysogonus makes the construct more powerful as, should they find Roscius guilty, the jurors become complicit in Chrysogonus' plan. Considering Chrysogonus' political connections and the reach of his influence, this is a bold play by Cicero.

iudices: Cicero regularly addresses the panel of jurors when giving a speech in a law court. This gives the suggestion of conversation and familiarity which in turn allows Cicero to seem more trustworthy and persuasive.

in alienam pecuniam: Cicero's use of **pecuniam** here, and later in the passage, refers to the entire estate and inheritance.

quoniam ... quoniamque: Cicero sets out the two strands of his attack on Chrysogonus reinforced by the anaphora of **quoniam** – 1. he has stolen another's property with no legal right (**nullo iure**) and 2. Sextus Roscius' life now poses an obstacle to him. Cicero heightens the drama of his assertions by the use of aggressive language (**invaserit**) and of tautology (**obstare atque officere**). Cicero's use of the subjunctive following **quoniam** is also interesting as it suggests these are the reasons Chrysogonus himself would offer if he were to speak directly to the jurors. The tone is therefore ironic – *since he says he has ... he demands that you. ...* **pecuniae** is dative following **obstare** and **officere**.

sese ... non arbitratur ... posse: accusative and infinitive for indirect speech – *he does not think that he is able ...*, the subject of the sentence is still Chrysogonus.

hoc incolumi: ablative absolute – *while this man is safe*. **hoc** refers to Roscius. **incolumi** may also be rendered *alive*.

damnato et eiecto: a further ablative absolute referring to Roscius – *but with him condemned and driven out . . .* **eiecto** is unclear as the penalty (which Cicero will go on to discuss later in the speech) is death, not exile (although Cicero may be referring to voluntary exile, a choice taken by many Romans in the face of likely condemnation). Regardless of the precise meaning, certainly Roscius would make no further claim on the property after a guilty verdict.

quod adeptus est per scelus, id per luxuriam: the contrast here is striking – Chrysogonus wishes to use his criminality to fund an extravagant lifestyle. Both **quod** and **id** refer to the gains he has made from the purchase of Roscius' inheritance. **scelus** hints at the illegal addition of the elder Roscius' name to the proscription lists.

hunc . . . scrupulum . . . ut evellatis, postulat: again, the word order can be a little confusing. Cicero has delayed the main verb (**postulat**) beyond the indirect command it introduces (**ut evellatis**) – *he demands that you pluck out this anxiety*. The repetition of **postulat** emphasizes the choice which faces the jurors.

ut . . . adiutores vos profiteamini: Cicero finishes this section with a final, blunt assertion: by convicting Roscius, the jurors declare themselves Chrysogonus' accomplices and demonstrate their willingness to condone criminal acts conducted using political power. **ut . . . profiteamini** is again reliant on **postulat** and may require a conjunction when translating into English – *he demands that you pluck out . . . and confess yourselves. . . .*

7

si vobis aequa et honesta postulatio videtur: referring back to Chrysogonus' imagined demand to relieve him of his anxiety. The tone is clearly sarcastic.

ego contra brevem postulationem adfero: Cicero's response is a proposition of his own. **contra** should be taken in its adverbial sense (*in* *reply, in turn*) while **brevem**, a term regularly used by Cicero in relation to points of his own making, not only suggests brevity, but also straightforwardness.

quo modo mihi persuadeo: literally – *by which manner I persuade myself*. Consider – *so it seems to me . . . / so I am convinced. . . .*

primum a Chrysogono ... deinde a vobis: a neatly paralleled construction – Cicero's request comes in two parts, a request to Chrysogonus and a request to the jurors (both of which are then broken down further). **peto** introduces the indirect commands and should be used with each of the subjunctives which follows.

- **a Chrysogono peto ut ... contentus sit ...**
- **peto ... ne petat ...**
- **peto ... a vobis ... ut ... resistatis ...**
- **peto ... ut ... levetis ...**
- **peto ... ut ... propulsetis**

The request to Chrysogonus is balanced, containing two elements he *should* be content with (**pecunia fortunisque nostris** – certainly ironic) and two elements he *should not* seek (**sanguinem et vitam**). Cicero's use of **nostris** demonstrates the threat is broader than this single case. The request to the jurors, formed as a tricolon, gradually increases in intensity – *resist ... ease ... drive out*. Cicero neatly demonstrates that the specifics of the case are relevant to his whole audience (**quod in omnes intenditur**).

audacium sceleri resistatis, innocentium calamitatem levetis: expertly balanced three-word phrases – the initial word in each is an adjective in the genitive standing in for a noun – *the criminal activity of daring men ... the misfortune of innocent men. . . .* Again, Cicero looks to broaden the appeal of his message as his use of the plural highlights that this is not just about Chrysogonus or Roscius.

8

quod si: *but if* . . .

causa criminis: **causa** functions as the noun here – *a reason for the charge / grounds for the accusation*. Phrased as a chiasmus with **facti suspicio** which follows.

aut quaelibet denique vel minima res: a slightly complex phrase – **quaelibet** agrees with **res** but should be taken separately – *or anything finally, even the smallest thing.* . . .

illi: *those men*, i.e. the prosecution.

non nihil tamen in deferendo nomine secuti: **secuti** is syncopated (**secuti** [esse]) following **videantur** which precedes it. The object of **secuti** is **non nihil** – *that they have followed not nothing*, i.e. that they have been led by anything at all. The use of litotes (deliberate understatement, particularly using a negative) **non nihil** emphasizes just how unlikely Cicero feels it is that the prosecution has anything upon which to base the charge. **in deferendo nomine** is a legal term meaning *in bringing the indictment*.

eam praedam: i.e. the estate of Sextus Roscius the Elder.

quicquam aliud causae: *anything else of reason*, i.e. *any other reason*.

quin illorum libidini Sex. Rosci vita dedatur: **quin** follows the negative **non recusamus** which precedes it – *that the life of Sextus Roscius be given up to.* . . .

ut eis ne quid desit: *so that nothing [not anything] might be lacking to those people* – **eis** refers to Chrysogonus, Titus and Magnus, and the prosecution. **ut** follows **nisi** – *except so that.* . . .

velut cumulus accedat: Cicero views the condemnation of Sextus Roscius as the culmination of Chrysogonus' crimes. **cumulus** is often translated as *heap* but can mean *crown*. **accedat** usually means *approach* but in this context means *be added*.

nonne cum multa indigna tum vel hoc indignissimum est vos idoneos habitos: while complex on first sight, the component parts of this phrase are more straightforward:

- **nonne ... hoc indignissimum est** – *surely this is the most outrageous thing ...*
- **cum multa indigna** – *among many outrages ...*
- **vos idoneos habitos [esse]** – *that you are considered suitable ...* **habitos** is a syncopated perfect passive infinitive form as part of an indirect statement.

per quorum sententias iusque iurandum: *through whose judgements and the swearing of oaths*. **quorum** refers to **vos** in the previous phrase and, since Cicero addresses the jurors, may be more easily translated as *your*. **sententias iusque iurandum** form a hendiadys and should be taken as a single idea – *judgements made under oath*.

quod antea ipsi scelere et ferro adsequi consuerunt: **quod** refers back to **id adsequantur** (*that they might acquire this*) which in turn refers to consolidating the theft of property with Roscius' condemnation. The connecting relative leads into the contrast – *a thing which they themselves were previously accustomed to attain through. . . .* Cicero heightens the threat in the case through his assertion that the courts are now being used to legitimize criminal activity.

qui ex civitate in senatum propter dignitatem: the first of two parallel phrases emphasizing the responsibility borne by the jurors. The phrase is reliant on **delecti estis** which follows – *you who ... have been chosen ...* **ex senatu in hoc consilium ... propter severitatem** works in the same fashion.

ab his hoc postulare homines sicarios atque gladiatores: **ab his** referring to the jurors – *from these men ...*, **homines sicarios atque gladiatores** is accusative as part of an indirect statement still relying on **indignissimum est** (the second of two rhetorical questions) – *[the most outrageous thing is] that these murderous men and gladiators ask this. . . .*

non modo ut supplicia vitent ... verum etiam ut spoliis ... ornati auctique discedant: a second climax using a rhetorical question. Having previously emphasized the responsibility of the jurors to avoid abuse of the court system, Cicero makes plain the aims of the prosecution, to leave the court without penalty and enriched. The balanced construction **non modo ... verum etiam** further emphasizes the outrageous nature of their aims.

9

neque satis me commode dicere: the first of three statements (*tricolon*) which are reliant on the indirect statement **me ... posse ...** (introduced by **intellego**) which follows – *I understand that I am able....* The repetition (*anaphora*) of **neque satis** signals a new phrase, each increasing in its severity – *to speak ... to lament ... to cry aloud.* Cicero regularly highlights his lack of ability or the restrictions placed upon him in order to seek the indulgence of his listeners.

nam commoditati ingenium, gravitati aetas, libertati tempora: a second tricolon which elaborates on the previous one. The structure is balanced using a parallel construction in each of the three phrases – a dative followed by a nominative on each occasion. Each phrase is reliant on **sunt impedimento** which follows:

- **ingenium ... aetas ... tempora sunt impedimento** – *my abilities ... my age ... the times are an impediment.* **impedimento** is a predicative dative (*a source of impediment*).
- **commoditati ... gravitati ... libertati** – *to what is appropriate ... to impressiveness : ... to freedom.*

Cicero's choice of abstract nouns in the dative is difficult to render in English without additional phrases such as *to speaking with* – *My abilities are an impediment to speaking appropriately, my age [an impediment] to speaking impressively, the times [in which we live are an impediment] to speaking freely.* The concise nature of the Latin would have allowed Cicero to express each element of the tricolon with particular force.

natura pudorque meus: hendiadys – *my nature and modesty = my natural modesty*.

vestra dignitas et vis adversariorum et Sex. Rosci pericula: **vestra** refers to the jurors. Cicero suggests he is surrounded by challenges, not only because of his own character and youth but also because of the intimidating nature of the jurors, the strengths of his opponents and because of what is at stake here (**pericula** referring to the outcome of the case if Roscius is found guilty).

vos oro atque obsecro: after sufficient build-up, Cicero makes his final plea to the jurors (expressed tautologically for extra emphasis) – **ut attente ... audiatis** that they listen carefully and with an additional level of indulgence considering the obstacles which face him.

10

fide sapientiaque vestra fretus: Cicero lays out his expectations to the jurors – their positive approach has given him the encouragement he needs. A form of flattery, demonstrating Cicero's belief in their integrity. **fide** is also suggestive of the oath the jurors have taken.

plus oneris sustuli: **oneris** is partitive genitive following **plus** – *more of a burden*. Consider *a greater burden*. Cicero refers to the weight of responsibility of defending the case.

si vos aliqua ex parte adlevabitis: for future conditionals Latin uses the future tense – *if you will lighten* whereas English tends to use the present – *if you lighten*. **aliqua ex parte** is used adverbially – *to some extent, in some way, to some degree*. Cicero hopes the jurors' indulgence will take the pressure off him (and that they will be more receptive).

ut potero: *as much as I am able* – again, the future does not translate well into English.

id quod non spero: a little aside to qualify **deserar** which follows – *a thing which I do not expect*. In negative phrases, **spero** is often used of expectation rather than hope.

quod si ... non potero: *but if I am not able. ...* Again, the present tense for **potero** is more natural in English.

opprimi me onere offici malo: the construction after **malo** is accusative and infinitive indirect statement – *I would rather that I am. ...* Cicero presents himself as the virtuous defence lawyer, willing to risk all for the sake of defending a cause which he knows to be right.

quam id ... aut ... abicere aut ... deponere: the remainder of this sentence may seem a little overwhelming but, when stripped back it is relatively straightforward. Cicero lays out the alternatives to defending the case despite the challenges – *than either to cast it aside ... or to give up*. **id** refers to the case and is the object of **abicere** and **deponere**.

quod mihi cum fide semel impositum est: again, Cicero makes a nod to his own virtue – others have entrusted the case to him and to fail to follow through would be a betrayal. The two hypothetical reasons **propter perfidiam** and **propter infirmitatem animi** would bring about his disgrace in the public eye.

11

magno opere ... quaeso: **magno opere** is functioning adverbially with **quaeso** – literally *I beseech you with great effort* – consider *I beseech you earnestly*.

M. Fanni: Marcus Fannius was the praetor acting as judge presiding over the court at the time the speech was given. Cicero makes his appeal directly to him, encouraging him to show the same character as he has done previously. Again, Cicero's flattery of Fannius is an attempt to bring him on side. **Fanni** is second declension vocative (where the noun has an 'i' in the stem).

ut, qualem te iam antea populo Romano praebuisti ... impertias: Cicero breaks the indirect command (**ut ... impertias** – *that you bestow*) with a relative clause (**qualem te ... praebuisti** – *the sort of man you showed yourself*). Cicero is referring to Fannius' conduct in an earlier case.

cum huic eidem quaestioni iudex praeesses: as suggested above, Fannius has presided over this court on a previous occasion.

talem te: paired with **qualem te** which precedes it, literally – *the sort of man you showed yourself ... bestow such a man.* You may wish to consider combining the two into a single phrase – *bestow upon us the same sort of man as you were. ...*

omnium mortalium: Cicero raises the stakes through his choice of vocabulary. Whereas previously a crowd of men, the exspectations and desires he attributes to *all mortals*. Although directly equivalent to *homines*, the term feels much more powerful in that it suggests the case is relevant to all and that the expectations in terms of the outcome are universal.

acria ac severa: tautology emphasizing Cicero's assertion that the judgements in this case cannot be seen to be lacking in strength.

longo intervallo: ablative absolute – *after a considerable pause.*

inter sicarios: the court in which this case is being tried is the *quaestio inter sicarios* established under the *Lex Cornelia de sicariis et veneficis* ('The Cornelian Law concerning assassins and poisonings') of 81 BC, although the court actually dealt with all murders. As such, Cicero is using the technical term to refer to the sitting of a court of this type. The phrase **iudicium inter sicarios** might, therefore, be translated as simply a *murder trial*.

committitur: although often *to commit* or *entrust*, *committere* has the sense of bringing together and thus, of events and often in the passive, means to *hold*, *begin* or *undertake*.

cum interea: when paired with **interea, cum** regularly takes the indicative meaning *whereas / even though at this time*.... Cicero is highlighting the disparity between the sitting of the court and murders taking place. As the first trial of this kind in a significant time, the status of the case is elevated but this does not mean other murders have not taken place!

omnes ... sperant: Cicero presents himself as the voice of the people, offering seemingly common-sense expectations. This puts pressure on the jurors to accept his arguments more readily. Combined with the way he describes these expectations, that the court be capable of acting in the face of **manifestis maleficiis cotidianoque sanguine** – *clear wickedness and everyday bloodshed* – makes it very difficult for anyone to argue a different proposition. The use of the ablative absolute **te praetore** – *while you are praetor* – puts further pressure on Marcus Fannius to demonstrate his moral intergrity.

futuram: syncopated future infinitive (**futuram** [esse]) forming an indirect statement with **hanc quaestionem** following **sperant** – *[everyone] hopes that this trial will be*....

12

qua vociferatione: this relative clause introduced by the ablative pronoun modifies **ea** which follows. This in turn is the object of **nos ... utimur** (in the ablative as *utor* takes an ablative) – *we are using the cry which*....

qui causam dicimus: modifies **nos** in the previous phrase – *we who are pleading the case*....

petimus ... ut ... vindicetis ... ut ... resistatis ... ut ... cogitetis: a string of clauses following the main verb. All are indirect commands following **petimus** (*we seek that you avenge ... that you resist ... that you consider ...*).

nisi in hac causa, qui vester animus sit, ostendetis: a conditional clause following the final indirect command **ut ... cogitetis, nisi ... ostendetis ...** *that you consider unless you show ...*, **qui vester animus sit** is an indirect question following **ostendetis** – *what your mindset is. ...*

eo prorumpere hominum cupiditatem et scelus et audaciam: indirect statement following **ut ... cogitetis** using an accusative and infinitive construction – *that men's desire and criminality and boldness will break forth to such an extent. ...* The force of the tricolon **cupiditatem ... scelus ... audaciam** is heightened by Cicero's use of polysyndeton **et ... et. ...** The use of the present tense **prorumpere** is unusual and considered spurious by some commentators – it is possible Cicero is using it for rhetorical effect emphasizing the immediacy of the problem.

ut non modo clam, verum etiam hic ... caedes futurae sint: Cicero reaches the climax of his thought process with a result clause reliant on **eo** in the previous phrase – *that there will be slaughter not only ... but also. ...* Cicero is particularly keen on ensuring that cases which he takes on are presented as a threat not only to the individuals involved but also to the state. Cicero's argument is that if jurors fail to defend an innocent man against the threat posed by powerful individuals within the state, they will become emboldened to the point that criminality becomes an open part of society.

ante tribunal tuum ... ante pedes vestros ... inter ipsa subsellia: Again, Cicero looks to heighten the impact of his words through the use of a tricolon, this time supported by anaphora (**ante ... ante ...**), and through a hyperbolic presentation of murder in the forum, before the jurors' feet and even among the benches of the courtroom. While it may seem Cicero is catastrophizing, there were indeed outbreaks of violence in the forum and in courtrooms during Cicero's lifetime. The **tribunal** was the raised platform in the forum on which the praetor had his seat when overseeing the court. The **subsellia** were the benches where the jurors and other officials sat.

13

ut id fieri liceat: *so that this may be allowed to happen*, i.e. so that murder may be committed without consequence (as laid out in the previous section). Cicero will expand on this theme by contrasting the plight of Sextus Roscius with the acts of his accusers throughout the remainder of this section, a rhetorical technique known as *antithesis*.

accusant ei ... causam dicit is: the first of four antitheses in this section. Each follows the same pattern immediately followed by a relative clause describing either the prosecution or Sextus Roscius.

quibus occidi patrem Sex. Rosci bono fuit: a possessive dative – *to whom it was a benefit that ...*, **bono** is a predicative dative (literally: *to whom it was a source of good*). This is a theme which Cicero makes use of several times in the speech (Sections 84 and 86). The concept, not of Cicero's invention, invites the jurors to question who profited by the crime (and is a readily accepted technique for criminal investigations today). In this instance, it is clear that Sextus Roscius' circumstances have only worsened since the death of his father.

qui hunc ipsum iugulare summe cupierunt ... cum praesidio venit: having drawn our attention to the relative fortunes of the parties involved, Cicero uses the third antithesis to focus on the danger to Sextus Roscius' life. Not only is he impoverished, he arrives at the court with a bodyguard (likely referring to friends accompanying Roscius to court) to preserve his very existence.

ne hic ibidem ante oculos vestros trucidetur: Cicero increases the drama once again (in a similar fashion to Section 12). The idea that Roscius' accusers would choose to murder him before the jurors is clearly hyperbolic but, nonetheless, focuses the audience's minds on the possibility.

quos populus poscit: *whom the people demand [be put on trial]* – this is a technique which Cicero uses in a number of other cases. Not only does he present the accusers as the guilty party but (through his assertion that it is the **populus** who desire their punishment) he also suggests that their guilt is universally acknowledged.

qui unus relictus ex illorum nefaria caede: again, a hyperbolic statement.

14

atque ut facilius intellegere possitis: *and so that you may be able to understand more easily. . . .* Cicero addresses the jurors directly signalling a shift to the *narratio* (an account of the facts) in the case.

ea quae facta sunt indigniora esse: **ea** is the accusative subject of an indirect statement following **intellegere** in the previous phrase. **quae facta sunt** (*which have been done*) describes **ea**.

quam haec sunt quae dicimus: Cicero highlights the limits of his descriptive powers to emphasize the severity of the situation – *than the things which we say are.* **quam** introduces the comparison following **indigniora** in the previous phrase.

quo facilius . . . cognoscere possitis: purpose clause introduced by **quo** the relative – literally *by which you might be able to recognize more easily*, consider *so that you might. . . .*

15

Sex. Roscius, pater huiusce: i.e. Sextus Roscius the elder.

municeps Amerinus fuit: a municipium was a free town, governed by local magistrates, made up of Roman citizens. As a member of this community, Cicero refers to the elder Sextus Roscius as a **municeps**.

cum genere . . . tum gratia: as a coordinated construction, **cum** and **tum** are paired to imply contrast – consider *while . . . also . . .* or *not only . . . but also . . .*

genere et nobilitate et pecunia: A tricolon of ablatives of respect – *in race and nobility and wealth*.

gratia atque hospitiis florens hominum nobilissimorum: *eminent through his friendship and ties with the most noble of men*. Although genitive, **hominum nobilissimorum** describes the style of these relationships and is more easily taken as *with*. The superlative **nobilissimorum**, and its positioning at the end of the phrase, highlights Cicero's outrage that such a man, who also had ties to the regime, should be proscribed in such a way.

cum Metellis, Serviliis, Scipionibus: the Metelli, Servilii and Scipiones were extremely prominent families in the Republic with long-standing histories and influence.

non modo hospitium, verum etiam domesticus usus et consuetudo: while **hospitium** implies ties of guest-friendship through obligation, Cicero's focus on **domesticus usus** and **consuetudo** is highly suggestive of the affection felt for the elder Sextus Roscius by the families mentioned.

gratia nomino: although the second appearance of **gratia** in this section, here it is used with the accompanying genitives meaning *for the sake of*.

vi ereptum: describing the **patrimonium** – *[his] inheritance snatched away by force*.

fama et vita innocentis ab hospitibus amicisque paternis defenditur: Cicero highlights the enduring family ties which defend Sextus Roscius to further emphasize the virtue of both the father and the son. Material possessions may be taken away by theft but reputation cannot. **innocentis** refers to Sextus Roscius the younger (*of an innocent man*) while **paternis** modifies both **hospitibus** and **amicis** – *the connections and friends of his father*.

16

hic cum omni tempore nobilitatis fautor fuisset: **hic** refers to Sextus Roscius the elder. Here Cicero attempts to build up his *optimate* credentials as a **fautor nobilitatis** (*defender of the nobility*).

tum hoc tumultu proximo: the **tumultu** to which Cicero refers is the civil war of 83–82 BC fought between Sulla and the Marians (led by Cinna) which led to Sulla's establishment as dictator and the proscriptions previously mentioned.

praeter ceteros in ea vicinitate: as well as *except*, **praeter** can also carry the meaning *beyond*. Here, Cicero points out the elder Sextus Roscius' role as the lead supporter of the Sullan cause in his locality.

eam partem: *that faction, that party* – i.e. Sulla's side.

opera, studio, auctoritate: a tricolon of ablatives – *through his efforts, his zeal and influence*.

propter quos ipse . . . numerabatur: *on account of whom he himself was considered* – i.e. to defend those whom he felt had assisted in his own social elevation.

victoria constituta est: Sulla's forces were victorious and Sulla appointed as dictator to settle the constitution. At the beginning of 80 BC Sulla resigned the dictatorship but remained consul and retained immense influence over the city at the time this speech was delivered.

cum proscriberentur homines: thousands of individuals were killed during the Sullan proscriptions after the war. The elder Roscius' circumstances (either status or location) would not have allowed him to escape the same fate had he been a genuine target.

erat ille Romae frequens atque in foro: as Cicero makes clear, however, the elder Roscius behaved in a manner which suggested nothing was wrong – for a man whose name had genuinely been added to the proscription lists to act in this way would have been lunacy.

in ore omnium: literally *in the face of all* – the idiom suggests that he was seen by everyone. Consider – *before the eyes of all*.

magis ut exsultare ... videretur quam timere: a result clause describing the impression made by Roscius' behaviour. The placement of **magis** is unhelpful and should be taken after **videretur** – *so that he seemed more to delight than to fear*. ...

ne quid ex ea calamitatis sibi accideret: fear clause following **timere** in the previous phrase. **ex ea** refers to his behaviour (*from this*) while **calamitatis** modifies **quid** (*something of calamity*). *Some calamity* is more natural.

17

cum duobus Rosciis Amerinis: Titus Roscius Magnus and Titus Roscius Capito (hereafter Magnus and Capito), both relatives of the elder Sextus Roscius.

quorum alterum sedere in accusatorum subselliis video: *one of whom I see ...*, Magnus is present in the court. Cicero draws attention to Magnus throughout the speech who is presumably there in the capacity of a witness.

alterum tria huiusce praedia possidere audio: *the other I hear ...* referring to Capito. Without naming him, Cicero has already demonstrated that Capito has benefitted significantly by the elder Roscius' death while the younger Roscius (**huiusce**) has been deprived of his property.

si tam cavere potuisset, quam: **tam** is paired with **quam** which follows – *if he had been able to be as much on his guard [against these hostilities] as*. ...

iniuria metuebat: **iniuria** in the ablative is used as an adverb – *[nor] was he unjustly afraid*. ...

nam duo isti sunt T. Roscii . . . homines eius modi: although a chunky phrase, when the subordinate clauses are removed it becomes clear that **sunt** should be kept until the end of the sentence – *for those two Roscii are men of this type. . . .*

alter plurimarum palmarum vetus ac nobilis gladiator habetur: Cicero revels in the gladiatorial imagery as it has connotations of criminality in his mind. **alter** refers to Capito. Although **vetus** and **nobilis** sound positive, Cicero is clearly trying to create a negative image of an experienced thug. **palmarum** refers to the palm wreaths given to winners in such contests and is intended to connote the many victories to his name. **habetur** is being used figuratively and should be taken as *considered* or *thought*.

hic . . . se ad eum lanistam contulit: **hic** refers to Magnus. Setting Capito (**eum**) up as Magnus' **lanistam** (which is in apposition to **eum**) and Magnus as the **tiro** allows Cicero to suggest excessive aptitude on Magnus' part for criminal activity as, by the end of the sentence, the pupil has surpassed the master.

quod sciam: *as far as I am aware* – this slight, ironic, aside brings into question Cicero's previous statement that Magnus is inexperienced and is suggestive of other crimes he may have committed.

18

cum hic Sex. Roscius esset Ameriae: **cum** is temporal to highlight the difference with Magnus which follows. **Sex. Roscius** refers to the younger Roscius. **Ameriae** is locative – *in Ameria*.

T. autem iste Roscius Romae: referring to Magus. The implication is clear – being in Rome, Magnus had much more opportunity to murder the elder Roscius.

cum hic filius: referring back to the younger Roscius.

voluntate patris: this is a particular point which Cicero plays on several times throughout the speech. The prosecution clearly suggests (although we do not have their words) that the younger Roscius was left behind to manage the farms as a punishment of sorts. Cicero's counterview is that Roscius' activities and the production of food was, to most Romans, a virtuous pursuit.

iste autem frequens Romae esset: the text is slightly uncertain here. As it stands, **iste** must refer to Magnus. As we have been told only moments earlier that Magnus was in Rome, some editors choose to insert **ipse** which could refer to the elder Roscius. **iste** does make sense, however, helping to reinforce the link between Magnus' presence in Rome and the death of the elder Roscius mentioned next.

occiditur ad balneas Pallacinas rediens a cena Sex. Roscius: the subject of **occiditur** is deliberately left to the end of the phrase for emphasis.

verum id . . . nisi perspicuum res ipsa fecerit: a slightly tricky phrase – *but unless the matter itself makes this clear*. **id** refers back to the suggestion that suspicion should fall on Magnus as he was actually present in Rome. **res** refers to Cicero's narration of events of the case (translators often opt to render **res** as *the facts of the case*). **fecerit** is future perfect as part of the conditional clause introduced by **nisi** but is usually reflected with a present tense in English.

quod adhuc est suspiciosum: Cicero acknowledges that this is just a theory and that Magnus' presence in Rome is what we might term circumstantial. He quickly encourages the jurors to look beyond this through his contrast of **suspiciosum** with **perspicuum** in the next phrase. **quod** relates to **id** – Cicero's assertion that Magnus is responsible.

hunc adfinem culpae iudicatote: the resolution of the conditional clause (apodosis). **iudicatote** is a future imperative (sometimes known as a permissive imperative) – *you may judge this man. . . .* **hunc** refers to the younger Sextus Roscius.

19

Ameriam nuntiat: *brings the news to Ameria*.

homo tenuis, libertinus, cliens et familiaris istius T. Rosci: Cicero's description of Mallius Glaucia is designed to create suspicion. **tenuis** suggests a man of low social status and, in Cicero's eyes, suceptible to bribery and manipulation. His status as **libertinus** suggests loyalty to another party and the description **cliens et familiaris** implies both ties of obligation and a close relationship with Magnus (**T. Rosci**).

domum non fili, sed T. Capitonis inimici: Cicero's point is strikingly obvious – a man carrying a message of the elder Roscius' death would surely bring it to his home, not that of his enemy.

et cum post horam primam noctis … primo diluculo nuntius … venit: at fifty-six Roman miles (about fifty miles) north of Rome, the messenger would have been travelling at significant speed to make it to Ameria by daybreak.

decem horis nocturnis sex et quinquaginta milia passuum cisiis pervolavit: it is rare to be offered such precision in a speech of this kind but, by including figures for both time and distance and being specific about the method of travel, Cicero makes his point loudly and clearly. **pervolavit** (literally *flew through*) adds further emphasis – Mallius Glaucia undoubtedly had reason to get there as quickly as possible. The plural **cisiis** suggests that fresh carriages were taken at points along the road to avoid having to stop.

exoptatum inimico nuntium: Cicero's accusation is pretty clear: it is not by chance that the elder Sextus Roscius died – it was actively desired.

cruorem inimici quam recentissimum telumque paulo ante e corpore extractum: Cicero brings his accusation to a gory climax – not enough for Mallius Glaucia to relay the news that the task had been completed but he needs to show it. The use of **quam recentissimum** (*as fresh as can be, still quite fresh*) to describe **cruorem** adds an extra layer of horror (both giving graphic detail and suggesting the messenger was motivated by the freshness of the kill). The mention of **telum** has created a hendiadys of sorts – the gore and the weapon are one and the same thing.

20

quadriduo quo: an abbreviation for **qudriduo** [a die] **quo** – *within four days of this*. . . .

ad Chrysogonum in castra L. Sullae … defertur: Cicero's argument takes a turn – this is not a family feud but involves the highest powers in the state. Lucius Sulla, as has already been mentioned, had won a civil war, held a dictatorship and was, at the time of this trial, consul. Cicero is careful not to associate Sulla with the crime itself (perhaps because of potential repercussions) but does not hold back when it comes to Chrysogonus.

nam fundos decem et tris reliquit: although normally translated as *farm*, fundus implies an estate of fields and farm buildings. To have the opportunity to buy thirteen at a bargain price is a significant prize.

Tiberim fere omnes tangunt: to have them bordering the Tiber just adds to the value of Roscius' estates.

huius inopia et solitudo commemoratur: Cicero is deliberately playing on the emotions of the jurors. The younger Roscius is undoubtedly not entirely without means at this point in the narrative but it suits Cicero's case to have him appear the helpless orphan preyed upon by those more powerful.

demonstrant … perfacile hunc hominem de medio tolli posse: **demonstrant** introduces an accusative (**hunc hominem**) and infinitive (**posse**) indirect statement but it is delayed by the **cum** clause (**cum pater huiusce Sex. Roscius**) which immediately follows – *they show that this man is able to be removed*. . . . As a phrase *tollere de medio* (used in a variety of idiomatic phrases) means *to be done away with*. **de medio** implies removal from the public eye (literally *from the middle of things*).

homo tam splendidus et gratiosus ... hominem incautum et rusticum et Romae ignotum: again, Cicero puts significant emphasis on the grandeur of the elder Sextus Roscius and his vulnerable son. If a man as well known as him can be killed off, how easy will it be to take out the son? The tricolon of adjectives (*unsuspicious, rustic and unknown at Rome*) describing the younger Roscius are, in many ways, virtues emphasizing his simpler existence.

ad eam rem operam suam pollicentur: the subject of this verb is unclear but presumably refers to an agreement (formalized at the beginning of the next section) between Magnus, Capito and Chrysogonus. Certainly, however, Cicero's narrative so far suggests the plot is not limited to these three alone.

21

ne diutius teneam: Cicero regularly implies that he is missing out information and passing over details out of consideration to the jurors. The effect of this is, naturally, to suggest that there is considerably more he could be saying. *vos* should be implied to complete the phrase – *so that I do not detain [you] any longer*. . . .

societas coitur: although **societas** suggests a formal partnership, Cicero really means a plot to remove the younger Sextus Roscius. **coitur** is the passive form of *coeo* and with partnerships of this kind can be taken as *is formed* or *is entered into*.

cum nulla iam proscriptionis mentio fieret: the force of **cum** is concessive here – *although there was no longer mention of proscription*. The threat of proscription has now been removed from the general populace – Cicero invites his audience to ponder why the elder Sextus Roscius should find himself subject to it.

qui antea metuerant: *those who had feared before* – further evidence that Roscius, who has survived the previous purges, should not have any reason to fear proscription. The situation has changed and people are returning to the city.

in tabulas: *into the records [of those proscribed]* – formal records of proscription lists were kept after the event. You may wish to translate **tabulas** as *the proscription lists*.

manceps fit Chrysogonus; tria praedia vel nobilissima Capitoni propria traduntur: again, Cicero focuses on the closeness of Chrysogonus and the two Roscii to the events. **nobilissima** and **propria** both describe **tria praedia** (three farms – an interesting choice of vocabulary considering its similarity to the word for plunder *praeda*). **nobilissima** should be taken as *most splendid* (since farms are objects) and **propria** shows Capito's ownership of them (*as his own*).

iste T. Roscius nomine Chrysogoni . . . impetum facit: again referring to Magnus. Although military in tone, in this context **impetum facit** means *seized* or *took hold of*.

haec omnia . . . imprudente L. Sulla facta esse certo scio: whether Cicero is sincere in his statements about Sulla is impossible to say. Regardless, his position is clear on the surface: Sulla should not be tarnished by Chrysogonus' actions. **L. Sulla** is ablative agreeing with **imprudente**, an ablative absolute within the indirect statement – *I know for certain that all these things were done while Lucius Sulla was unaware.*

22

neque enim mirum: *nor is this is a surprise* – Cicero refers back to his statement at the end of the previous section that he is certain Sulla could not have knowledge of Chyrsogonus' actions. The remainder of this section is dedicated to demonstrating the great weight of responsibility on Sulla's shoulders and that it is unsurprising that a matter of this kind passed him by.

cum eodem tempore: the first of five **cum** clauses in this section, each one designed to demonstrate a different pressure facing Sulla. The verbs within these clauses are all subjunctive but are in the present tense demonstrating the ongoing nature of these pressures.

quae praeterita sunt: *which have passed* – Cicero is referring to the events of the recent civil war and Sulla's victory.

pacis constituendae rationem: a nod to Sulla's official responsibilities. Under the *Lex Valeria* of 82 BC, Sulla was made dictator *legis scribendae et rei publicae constituendae* ('for writing the laws and re-establishing the Republic'). **pacis constituendae** follows **rationem** and is subject to gerundival attraction. When translating, **pacis** should be taken as the object of **constitudendae** – *for establishing peace*. **rationem** although conventionally translated as *judgement* or *reason* may be better taken as *authority* here.

belli gerendi potestatem: again, gerundival attraction – *the power of waging war*.

unus omnia gubernet: a figurative use of **gubernet** which literally means *steer a ship* (*gubernator* is a helmsman). Cicero makes use of the *ship of state* metaphor in other speeches.

ut respirare libere non possit: hyperbolic but effective. Cicero imagines the responsiblity of managing the Roman state as so weighty that it becomes a physical impediment.

occupationem eius observent: this is a difficult phrase and is perhaps more easily rendered by taking **occupationem** as a verb phrase in English – *they watch him so deeply engrossed in his work. . . .*

ut . . . aliquid huiusce modi moliantur: *to undertake something of this kind* – the purpose clause is interrupted by the subordinate clause (**simul atque ille despexerit**). Through **aliquid huiusce modi** Cicero refers to the abuse of power which led to the proscription of the elder Roscius and this trial.

huc accedit quod: *added to this is the fact that. . . .*

quamvis ille felix sit: Cicero is engaging in word play here – Sulla took the name *Felix* after his victory in the civil war. Undoubtedly he is **felix** both by name and by nature.

in magna familia: it is easy for us as modern readers to forget just how enormous a wealthy Roman's household could be. Aristocratic Romans may have had control over hundreds or, in some cases, thousands of individuals. Cicero's point does have some validity, however, when one considers quite how close Chrysogonus was to Sulla it seems less plausible.

qui neminem neque servum neque libertum improbum habeat: Cicero reminds us of Chrysogonus' status as a former slave – despite his present wealth and influence, this would have been a source of disdain from aristocratic Romans.

23

interea iste T. Roscius, vir optimus: Cicero attempts to change gear and bring the narrative more vividly to his audience through his use of **interea**. Many of the following verbs are in the present tense to reinforce this. **iste T. Roscius** refers again to Magnus while his description of him as **vir optimus** is clearly sarcastic.

in praedia huius invadit: as in Section 21 (**impetum facit**), Cicero's choice of verb (**invadit**) has a very aggressive, military tone.

hunc miserum, luctu perditum: again, Cicero turns to pity as a tool to defend Roscius. He is weak and vulnerable, having just lost his father, in the face of a violent attack by his father's enemy.

omnia paterno funeri iusta solvisset: although usually *release* or *set free*, *solvere* can mean to fulfil actions, particularly those which are done through obligation (such as completion of vows or religious rites). Roman funerals could go on for as long as nine days after the body was buried – the *pathos* (appeal to emotion) is clear here – Roscius did not even have the opportunity to complete the rites for his father before being driven from his home.

nudum eicit domo: undoubtedly hyperbolic but the image of the naked man thrown from his home is both dramatic and compelling.

atque focis patriis disque penatibus ... exturbat: Cicero continues his focus on Roscius' suffering. Having lost his father, he now loses his father's legacy, the paternal hearth. **disque penatibus** often appears in this formula and should be translated as *penates* or *household gods*.

qui in sua re fuisset egentissimus: the subjunctive **fuisset egentissimus** should be taken as *who had been very poor* or *since he had been very poor*. Cicero uses the subjunctive here to express cause (Magnus is poor and therefore will be lavish when he obtains money). **in sua re** – *in his own affairs, by his own means*.

ut fit: aside – *as is the case, as happens*.

in aliena: shorthand for *another's property*.

clam de medio: *in secret from the public*, i.e. *out of the public eye*. Similar to Section 20 (**de medio tolli posse**).

24

usque eo visum est indignum, ut: **usque** and **eo** should be taken together suggesting how **indignum** the people of Ameria found the situation and leading naturally into the result clause which follows – *this seemed so intolerable that....*

multa ... ante oculos versabantur: literally *many things came before their eyes* – i.e. *they saw many things*.

crudelissima: agreeing with **mors hominis** earlier.

praedo iste nefarius: Magnus (named at the end of this section).

ne iter quidem ad sepulcrum patrium: it was standard practice, in the event that a family estate changed hands, to grant access to any tombs on the land to the remaining members of the family as part of the sale. Without any such sale having been agreed in this case, the younger Roscius has even lost the ability to freely access his father's tomb.

possessio, furta, rapinae, donationes: Cicero climaxes with an asyndetic and, to some extent, tautological list of the crimes perceived by the people of Ameria. **possessio** implies a violent seizure (a taking possession of) as does **rapinae**, while **furta** (*thefts*, from fur, *a thief*) makes clear that the act was unlawful. **donationes** (*gifts, largess*) suggests the payment of bribes in order to avoid detection or obstruction during the act.

qui non audere omnia mallet: some editors read **audere** as *ardere* – *who did not prefer to burn everything*. While this level of violence might suit Cicero's attempt to suggest the strength of feeling, considering what follows (a delegation to Sulla), it is clear that this level of direct action is not what Cicero has in mind. As such, **audere** seems a more fitting choice – *who did not prefer to risk everything.* . . .

in Sex. Rosci . . . bonis iactantem se: **bonis** is separated from **in** by the genitive (**Sex. Rosci**) and a subordinate clause – *on the property of Sextus Roscius*. **iactantem se** is a figurative expression (literally *throwing himself around*) which means *boasting, bragging*, or *making a display*. The sight of Magnus showing off is too much for people to bear.

dominantem: *lording it over*.

25

decurionum decretum statim fit: the *decuriones* are the members of the local senate of Ameria which, as a municipium, is populated with Roman citizens but has a level of independence from Rome. The *decuria*, or local senate, was usually made up of 100 men and then divided into groups of ten which gave rise to the name.

decem primi: *the ten leading men* – as the *decuria* is split into groups of ten, these are the leaders of the individual groups.

doceantque eum: although *doceo* is conventionally translated as *I teach*, it can also be used to suggest *inform* or *notify*.

qui vir Sex. Roscius fuerit: *what sort of man Sextus Roscius had been* – **fuerit** is perfect subjunctive as part of an indirect question.

de istorum scelere et iniuriis: *concerning the crime and injustices of those men*. **istorum** refers collectively to Magnus, Capito and Chrysogonus. **scelere** and **iniuriis** are tautological and could be taken as a hendiadys – *the unjust crime of those men*.

orent, ut ... conservatas velit: **orent** continues the run of present subjunctives as part of the indirect command reliant on **ut** in the first line (like **proficiscantur, doceant** and **conquerantur**) but then introduces a further indirect command – *and to beg him to....* **velit** is tricky here as its conventional meaning (*want*) does not quite fit – *ensure* or *see to it that* may be better renderings.

[decretum decurionum.]: at this point the decree of the senate of Ameria is read out to the court as evidence.

id quod iam ante dixi: *that which I said previously* – Cicero is referring to his assertion (which he will repeat here) that Sulla was unaware of the actions taken against Roscius.

ne ad Sullam adirent: negative indirect command – *not to approach Sulla*. Chrysogonus is using his influence to fob off the embassy with empty promises.

pollicerentur: purpose following **qui** – *and to promise that....* **Chrysogonum** is the subject of the indirect statement which follows.

26

usque adeo autem ille pertimuerat, ut: similar to **usque eo** in Section 24, **usque adeo** should be taken as a phrase leading into the result clause which follows – *he, however, had been so scared that ....*

mori mallet, quam ... Sullam doceri: **mallet** has two structures which follow.

- **mori mallet**: a simple infinitive – *he preferred to die* . . . .
- **quam . . . Sullam doceri**: accusative and infinitive indirect statement – *than that Sulla be informed* . . . .

homines antiqui: referring to people, **antiqui** means *old fashioned*, *simple* or *honest*. Their values are of those of simpler times (which puts them at a disadvantage when dealing with Chrysogonus and his crew).

qui ex sua natura ceteros fingerent: although *fingo* usually means *I touch* or *grasp*, it can be used figuratively referring to thoughts and ideas meaning *I imagine* or *suppose*. Here *who judged others* seems the most straightforward rendering. **ex sua natura** is a slightly tricky phrase (literally *from their own nature*) – consider *by their own standards*. We should not judge the delegation from Ameria for allowing themselves to be fobbed off – Cicero's suggestion is that they are men of high moral standing who anticipate others to be men of honour as well. Unfortunately, they are wrong in this instance.

ille confirmaret sese . . . exempturum: **ille** refers to Chrysogonus while **confirmaret** leads into an accusative and infinitive indirect statement relating back to him – *he confirmed that he would remove* . . . .

cumque id ita futurum T. Roscius Capito . . . appromitteret: the **cum** clause contains a new subject (**T. Roscius Capito**) while **appromitteret** leads into a further indirect statement, the subject of which is **id**.

- **cumque . . . T. Roscius Capito . . . appromitteret** – *and when T. Roscius Capito also promised* . . . .
- **id ita futurum [esse]** – *that this would be in this way* (i.e. *he promised that this would happen*). **esse** should be supplied with the future participle **futurum** to create the future infinitive.

re inorata: ablative absolute – *with the matter unheard / unspoken*, i.e. *without the chance to make their case*.

rem differre cotidie ac procrastinare isti coeperunt: the subject of **coeperunt** is Chrysogonus, Capito and the remainder of those who met the delegation from Ameria.

lentius nihil agere: while **lentius** would normally be rendered *more slowly*, with people it can be taken as *more unconcerned* or *more indifferent*. The sense is that with the pressure off, they have no interest in following through on their assurances. The infinitive **agere** (along with **deludere, parare** and **arbitrari** which follow) is reliant on **coeperunt**.

id quod facile intellectum est: a slight aside from Cicero – *as* (literally *that which*) *was easily recognized* . . . .

neque sese arbitrari posse . . . obtinere: as mentioned above, **arbitrari** is reliant on **coeperunt** earlier in the section. This then introduces an accusative and infinitive indirect statement (**sese . . . posse**) – *they began to think that they were not able to keep possession of* . . . .

domino incolumi: ablative absolute – *while the master was unharmed*.

27

quod hic simul atque sensit: **quod** is a connecting relative referring to the decision made at the end of Section 26. **hic** refers to the younger Sextus Roscius. **simul atque** is a variant of *simulatque* (*as soon as*) – *As soon as he noticed this* . . . .

de amicorum cognatorumque sententia: following a standard formula, Cicero expresses the opinion of Roscius' friends and relatives in a way which is recognizable to his audience. Such important family decisions would be brought before a *consilium cognatorum et amicorum*. **de** can be used to express cause – *by the advice of his friends and relatives* . . . .

ad Caeciliam, Nepotis sororem, Baliarici filiam: the text is uncertain here, some editions list Caecilia as **Nepotis sororem** and others only state that she was **Baliarici filiam**. It is possible that the additional detail was given as an explanatory note and not a part of the original speech. Both are retained here. **Caeciliam** refers to Caecilia Metella, one of the Late Republic's best known Roman matrons, a member of the extremely influential Caecilii Metelli. Caecilia was the daughter of Quintus Caecilius Metellus Baliaricus (**Baliarici filiam**), who received his cognomen as a result of his conquest of the Balearic Islands, and the sister of Quintus Caecilius Metellus Nepos (**Nepotis sororem**), who was consul in 98 BC. That Roscius is able to seek refuge with a noble woman of such standing shows the extent of his father's influence and connections.

qua pater usus erat: although usually *I use*, *utor* also has a further meaning *be friendly with* or *be intimate with*. As *utor* takes the ablative, the relative **qua** is the object of **usus erat** – *with whom his father had been friendly*.

quasi exempli causa: *as if to serve as a model* – Cicero focuses on the perceived virtues those willing to support Roscius display. Like the delegation sent to Chrysogonus (**homines antiqui**), in Caecilia can be seen **vestigia antiqui offici** (*traces of old-fashioned duty*) marking her out as a woman of upstanding morality. Her capacity to provide an example of such virtue to others emphasizes her calibre further.

ea Sex. Roscium ... recepit domum hospitique ... opitulata est: this substantial sentence is relatively straightforward when stripped back to its component parts. **ea** refers to Caecilia and is the subject of both **recepit** and **opitulata est** – *she welcomed Sextus Roscius into her home* and assisted her friend. The string of accusatives (**inopem, eiectum, expulsum, fugientem**) all describe **Sex. Roscium**, while the participles **oppresso** and **desperato** describe **hospiti** which is in the dative following **opitulata est** (with carries the sense *bring help to ...*). **hospiti** implies a tie of guest-frienship which the younger Roscius has inherited from his father.

eius virtute, fide, diligentia factum est: again, the pronoun **eius** refers to Caecilia while the nouns **virtute, fide, diligentia** are all instrumental ablatives (*by her courage, loyalty and diligence*). The impersonal **factum est** leads into **ut ... referretur** which follows (*it was made that he was considered ...*). You may wish to consider *it happened that ...* or *it turned out that ...*.

vivus in reos quam occisus in proscriptos: *a living man among the accused rather than dead among the proscribed.* The contrast is striking – without Caecilia, Roscius was so weak and his enemies so powerful

28

isti intellexerunt: referring to Magnus, Capito and Chrysogonus. **intellexerunt** leads into the accusative and infinitive indirect statement which follows.

vitam Sex. Rosci custodiri: the first of two indirect statements following **intellexerunt** – *after they understood that the life* . . . .

neque sibi ullam caedis faciendae potestatem dari: a second indirect statement – *that no opportunity was being given.* Although **potestatem** is usually translated as *power* it can, by extension, refer to *potential, chance* or *opportunity.*

consilium ceperunt: idiom – literally *they took a plan,* i.e. *they came up with a plan.*

ut nomen huius de parricidio deferrent: an *exegetic* ut clause explaining the nature of the plan – *they came up with a plan to....* **nomen huius ... deferrent** a technical phrase meaning *bring to court* or *accuse* (as in Section 8). **huius** modifies **nomen** (literally *report the name of this man,* i.e. *bring this man to court*). **de parricidio** is a reference to the charge – *on a charge of* . . . .

ut ad eam rem aliquem accusatorem veterem compararent: a second *exegetic* ut clause further elucidating their plans – *and to*. . . . **ad eam rem** should be taken as *for this matter* while **aliquem accusatorem veterem** refers to the experience of the advocate they planned to enlist to present their case – *some veteran prosecutor.* The implication is that whomever they employ, they will be experienced enough to make a case out of dubious or thin evidence.

in qua re nulla subesset suspicio: *in which matter there was no suspicion* – Cicero makes plain his view that there is no evidence in this case at all but, despite this, they have managed to obtain an advocate who is willing to speak on their behalf.

denique ut, quoniam crimine non poterant, tempore ipso pugnarent: a final ut clause (**ut...pugnarent**) laying out their plans. The subordinate clause **quoniam crimine non poterant** demonstrates the difficulty faced – without any evidence, they were unlikely to be able to secure a conviction. **tempore ipso pugnarent** (*they would fight making use of [the state of] the times*) introduces the idea, which will be expanded upon in the indirect speech which follows, that owing to the disruption to court business during the turbulence of the Sullan regime, a charge as serious as parricide will be seen as an opportunity to reassert the authority of the courts. A conviction is considerably more likely if they move quickly.

ita loqui homines: **loqui** is a historic infinitive functioning as a main verb. **homines** refers again specifically to Magnus, Capito and Chrysogonus – *the men spoke in this way....*

quod iudicia tam diu facta non essent: as a subordinate clause in indirect speech **facta...essent** is in the subjunctive.

condemnari eum oportere: the first of a series of accusative and infinitive constructions to form indirect speech following **ita loqui homines**.

- **condemnari eum oportere:** *that he should be condemned.*
- **patronos...defuturos:** *that defenders would be lacking* (supply **esse** after the future participle).
- **verbum esse facturum neminem:** *that no one would say (literally make) a word.*

qui primus in iudicium adductus esset: a further assertion that the conspirators felt they needed to move quickly in order to ensure that Roscius' trial was most inclined to go their way.

propter Chrysogoni gratiam: Chrysogonus' position and his association with the case (as the new owner of the land) would have been sufficient to put most advocates off speaking about this case. Cicero thus highlights even further the difficulties faced by Roscius. **gratiam** should be translated as *influence* here.

de bonorum venditione et de ista societate: i.e. about the public auction of the Elder Roscius' goods at auction (**de bonorum venditione**) a natural consequence of adding his name to the list of those proscribed. **de ista societate** refers to the partnership of Magnus, Capito and Chrysogonus.

ipso nomine parricidi et atrocitate criminis fore, ut: a final accusative and infinitive construction following **ita loqui homines** but the subject of the indirect statement is an impersonal *it* which accompanies **fore** (an alternative form of the future infinitive *futurum esse*). This construction is commonly followed by **ut** introducing a result clause – *[they said] that it would be in such a way that....* The use of a phrase such as *things would turn out in such a way that* may help but still feels slightly unnatural in English. Alternatively, **fore, ut** could be skimmed over and the result clause made the focal point of the sentence – *through the mere name of parricide and the atrocious nature of the crime he would be removed with no effort....*

29

cum cuperent: concessive cum clause – *although they desired it.*

non potuerunt occidere: the object of this phrase is **quem** which precedes it – *a man whom they [themselves] were unable to kill....*

eum iugulandum: the gerundive **iugulandum** implies purpose – *who should be killed*, i.e. *to kill*. The term implies a judicial execution rather than a criminal murder as sentence was often carried out by strangulation, the verb being derived from the noun *iugulum* – *the throat*.

29 cont.

quid primum querar ... ordiar ... petam? A series of deliberative questions (*what should I lament first ... from where should I begin ... what should I seek?*) using the present subjunctive. A common rhetorical technique which allows Cicero the opportunity to involve his audience and highlight his frustrations.

aut quod aut a quibus auxilium: **quod** agrees directly with **auxilium** (*what help*) while **a quibus** suggests the source of help – *what help [should I seek] or from whom?*

deorumne immortalium ... fidem implorem? A final deliberative question suggesting (somewhat hyperbolically) that, if Cicero cannot place his faith in the jury, then his only recourse is to the gods. **fidem,** usually *faith* or *reliance*, can also refer to a guarantee of security. It is sometimes used when invoking the divine. The question, introduced using the **-ne** of **deorumne immortalium**, would traditionally be followed by *an* to provide alternatives. Cicero has deliberately repeated the suffix as a form of anaphora to provide resonance and pace.

30

pater occisus nefarie, domus obsessa ... bona adempta, possessa, direpta ... vita infesta ... appetita: a striking list of the actions taken against the Younger Roscius. With only participles and no main verb, *est* (or *sunt* with **bona**) must be supplied – *His father was killed ..., his home besieged ...* etc. It is also worth noting that Cicero creates a crescendo through additional participles with **bona** and an extended clause following **vita**.

quid ... sceleris: the partitive genitive is common in Cicero – *what of crime,* i.e. *what crime.* The question is rhetorical.

haec aliis nefariis cumulant: *they crown these with other wicked acts.* Deliberately subverting the rhetorical question, Cicero emphasizes the lengths Magnus, Capito and Chrysogonus have gone to by, contrary to expectations, managing to attack him even further. He is, of course, referring to the criminal charge brought against Roscius which he is now defending. **adaugent** provides a tautology to emphasize the point further.

testes in hunc: *against him* – **hunc** refers to the Younger Roscius.

huiusce pecunia comparant: when paired with **hunc**, **huiusce** forms a polyptoton drawing attention to the irony that it is Roscius' own money that provides the resources for the case against him.

hanc condicionem misero ferunt: Cicero highlights the *Hobson's choice* with which the Younger Roscius is faced – submit to death at the hands of Titus or execution at the hands of the court. **misero** refers to the Younger Roscius – *to the wretched man*.

cervices T. Roscio dare: to give one's neck suggests 'to offer oneself up for death'. *cervix* often appears in the plural but should be taken as singular.

an insutus in culleum . . . vitam amittere: *or to lose his life sewn up in a sack* – Cicero refers to the traditional punishment given to those convicted of parricide in court (see Introduction). The punishment is extremely long-standing, having religious significance, but was also unlikely to have been enacted. If nothing else, a defendant was free to flee into exile at any point during the trial. Nevertheless, it suits Cicero's purpose to remind the jury of the horrific nature of the possible punishment.

patronos huic defuturos putaverunt; desunt: a familiar theme although with a slight twist – Cicero admits that Roscius is lacking in supporters (something to which he has also drawn attention at the beginning of the speech), although the most recent iteration of this argument (Section 28) implies that the conspirators were mistaken. Here, Cicero draws on it again but suggests that it is not mass support that is needed, just one man who is not enfeebled by cowardice.

A Level

qui ... dicat, qui ... defendat: **qui** + subjunctive to show purpose. Slightly complicated as **qui** is also the subject of **non deest** which follows – *a man to speak, a man to defend ... is not lacking* (referring to himself).

id quod in hac causa satis est: *that which is sufficient in this case*. **id quod** is used frequently as a conjunction in this manner. Cicero's confidence is brimming – the whole situation is so ludicrous that it only takes one person to stand up against it and the case will come tumbling down.

31

temere impulsus adulescentia fecerim: Cicero returns to a familiar theme – his youth and lack of experience. As an intransitive verb *facio* can mean *behave* or *act*, thus **temere ... fecerim** – *I have acted rashly*.

quoniam quidem: as a pair, **quidem** adds contrast to **quoniam** (adversative) – *since however, nevertheless since* ....

licet: in addition to its usual meaning (*it is permitted*), **licet** can be used as a conjunction meaning *even if, even though, despite*.

hercules: an exclamation – *by Hercules!* More commonly seen as *Hercule* or *Hercle*.

succurram ac subibo: the main verbs resolve the earlier clause introduced by **quoniam quidem** – *Since, however ... I shall I run to help and undertake them*.

certum est deliberatumque: an impersonal phrase – supply *mihi*. *It is resolved and determined for me*, i.e. *I have resolved and decided to* ....

quae ad causam pertinere arbitror: a slight aside – **quae** is accusative following **arbitror** as part of an indirect statement. *The things which I think pertain to the case* ....

non modo dicere, verum etiam libenter, audacter libereque dicere: the contrast exerted by **non modo ... verum etiam** is further strengthened by a tricolon of adverbs – *not only to say, but even to say gladly, boldly and freely*.

ut possit vim mihi maiorem adhibere metus quam fides: Cicero makes a display of Roman virtue here – under no circumstances will he allow fear to inhibit his pursuit of justice. The word order disguises the structure slightly – **metus** is the subject of **possit** (*so that fear might be able...*) which is then naturally followed by the infinitive **adhibere** (*to apply [greater force to me]*). **quam fides** then forms a comparison (*than good faith*).

32

quis tam dissoluto animo est: ablative of quality – *who is with so negligent a mind?*, i.e. *who has so negligent a mind* or *who is so lax in mind*. Rhetorical question.

qui ... possit: relative clause with the subjunctive functioning as a result clause – *that he could ...*.

patrem meum ... iugulastis: Cicero engages in a rhetorical technique known as prosopopoeia (a term derived from the Greek πρόσωπον, *prosōpon* – a mask or character in a drama). He takes on the role of the Younger Roscius and gives an imagined address to Magnus, Capito and Chrysogonus. The verbs which follow for the remainder of the section are all in the second person plural as a direct address to them. **iugulastis** is a syncopated form of *iugulavistis*.

occisum ... rettulistis: supply *him*. **occisum** functions as the object – *you reported him having been killed among the body of the proscribed*, i.e. *you reckoned him among the number of proscribed after he had been killed*. **proscriptorum** functions as a noun – *of proscribed [men]*.

patrimonium meum possidetis: as in Section 15, **patrimonium** refers specifically to the Younger Roscius' inheritance. The shift to the present tense for **possidetis** is important – Magnus, Capito and Chrysogonus still have possession of what is rightly his.

A Level

quid voltis amplius? An exclamation showing frustration – **voltis** is an alternative form of *vultis – you want.*

ad subsellia cum ferro atque telis venistis: ad subsellia refers to the benches of the courtroom – Magnus is actually present as an additional threat to the Younger Roscius.

aut iuguletis aut condemnetis? The two possible outcomes in Cicero's mind – either the Younger Roscius will be murdered by Magnus and Capito or condemned by the jurors (doing their dirty work for them). Most translators consider that for this final question Cicero speaks on his own behalf – *to kill or condemn Sextus Roscius?*

33–36: Cicero discusses the circumstances surrounding Gaius Fimbria, the most audacious man of recent history, who contrived the wounding of Quintus Scaevola at the funeral of Gaius Marius. He informs us that Fimbria then deigned to bring Scaevola to court to finish off the job which the violent assault on him had failed to do. This, he suggests, has more than a passing resemblance to the current case. The younger Roscius has been injured (in the form of the confiscation of his inheritance) and now is brought to trial to complete the attack on him. Should this be accepted just because the attack is by Chrysogonus?

In Section 35, Cicero embarks on the partitio, *a summary of the arguments which he will use to attack the prosecution for much of the remainder of the speech. He enumerates the obstacles, as he sees them, which face Roscius – Erucius' fabrication of a charge, Magnus and Capito's brazen audacity, and Chrysogonus' influence. The responsibility for tackling these, he says, should be distributed as follows: the challenge posed by Erucius is Cicero's to tackle, but the audacity of Magnus and Capito and Chrysogonus' influence over proceedings are the responsibility of the jurors.*

37

occidisse patrem Sex. Roscius arguitur: the infinitive is difficult to render – consider *of having killed*. Here, Cicero moves to the *propositio*, dealing directly with the prosecution's accusation.

quo uno maleficio: connecting relative – *in this single crime . . . .*

complexa esse: *to be encompassed* – while the verb *complector* is deponent, there is an active equivalent *complecto* which would allow the participle **complexa** to be used in a passive sense. Alternatively, some commentators cite this as an example of a deponent verb being used in the passive. Either way, the rendering is certainly passive – *be encompassed, be included*.

id quod praeclare a sapientibus dicitur: a general statement to support the question which follows – *that which is famously said by wise men*. **sapientibus** functions as a noun.

voltu saepe laeditur pietas: a statement of Republican values – *devotion is often damaged by a look*. The obligation of a son to respect his father is so strong that he can cause offence simply by a poorly judged facial expression.

quod supplicium satis acre reperietur: if we accept the above as true, which Cicero clearly intends us to do, there is no possible punishment appropriate for the murder of one's father. Cicero seeks to demonstrate his moral fibre and suggests that he would be a keen supporter of Roscius' death if he were indeed guilty.

pro quo mori ipsum: connecting relative – *for whom [they compelled] he himself to die* (referring to the hypothetical father). Further support for the devotion from a son towards his father required by the morals of the times.

iura divina atque humana: Cicero states his view as to the universal nature of this proposition. That a son should be willing to lay down his life for his father is a principle in both human and divine law. In such a statement, Cicero further emphasizes his belief, and that of any right-thinking person, that the Younger Roscius' punishment should be severe should he be found guilty. By extension, one can assume that Cicero would not be defending him if he suspected him to have committed such an act.

38

in hoc tanto, tam atroci, tam singulari maleficio: Cicero seeks to emphasize the outrageous nature of the charge against the Younger Roscius through a tricolon of adjectives. The anaphora of **tam** helps him in his aim.

quod ita raro exstitit: Cicero continues his focus on the magnitude of the crime. **ita** naturally leads into the result clause (**ut ... numeretur**) which follows – *which has happened so rarely that it was reckoned . . . .*

si quando auditum sit: it is possible that none of those listening had ever encountered an incident of parricide. **quando** is indefinite (*ever*) while **auditum sit** is impersonal – *if it was ever heard of . . . .*

portenti ac prodigi: a marvellous alliterative, tautological phrase which leaves the listener in no doubt of Cicero's opinion – the crime transcends the laws of nature. Both **portenti** and **prodigi** have a religious flavour meaning *portent* or *omen* but are also used to mean *monstrosity* or *unnatural act*.

quibus ... argumentis accusatorem censes uti oportere? the connecting relative **quibus** agrees with **argumentis**. Both are in the ablative as the object of **uti** (*utor* being followed by the ablative). The main verb **censes** introduces an indirect statement – *which arguments do you think the accuser ought to use*. Most translators take **accusatorem** as *you the accuser* since Cicero is posing this question directly to the prosecution.

C. Eruci: Gaius Erucius, the lead prosecution lawyer.

nonne et audaciam eius ... singularem ostendere: there is no main verb in this sentence, only an infinitive which relies on an implied sense of *ought* carried on from **oportere** in the previous question – *surely you ought to demonstrate both the extraordinary audacity of the man* ....

qui in crimen vocetur: referring to **eius** – *[of the man] who is called on the charge*. **vocetur** is present subjunctive as Cicero is talking in general terms (*the sort of man* ...) but this is redundant in English.

mores feros immanemque naturam et vitam ... deditam: further accusatives continuing the previous structure – *[surely you ought to demonstrate] his savage behaviours* etc.

et denique omnia ad perniciem profligata atque perdita: Cicero's final flourish in this section is a little ambiguous, relying on his listener's interpretation of **omnia** – *[you ought to demonstrate] everything overturned and squandered to utter ruin*. For Roscius to have committed such a heinous crime, he must be living a life of moral bankruptcy. **omnia** could be rendered as *his whole life* or *his entire character*.

quorum tu nihil ... contulisti: connecting relative – *of these things* (i.e. the list of qualities which Cicero suggests Erucius could call on) *you have brought forward nothing* ....

ne obiciendi quidem causa: *not even for the sake of slander* – **causa** here means *for the sake of* (not to be confused with *causa – the case*) and is followed by the gerund **obiciendi**. *obicio* can have a neutral tone (*defend, present*) but, as Erucius' role as prosecutor inherently involves substantiating his case, particularly when paired with **ne ... quidem**, Cicero undoubtedly means it to have a more aggressive tone – *slander, reproach*.

39

patrem occidit Sex. Roscius: not an admission of guilt by Cicero on behalf of his client. Rather, he sets up the premise with a view to dismantling it for the remainder of the section through a selection of hypotheses.

qui homo?: **qui** should be taken with the force of *qualis* here – *what sort of man is he?* A verb *to be* needs to be supplied. This begins an examination of Roscius' background (*probabile ex vita*) to establish whether there is any reason to believe he was the sort of person to commit such an act.

adulescentulus corruptus et ab hominibus nequam inductus? Cicero reaches for the usual stereotype of the young man influenced to carry out depraved acts. Roscius clearly does not fit this characterization. **nequam** is indeclinable but should be taken with **hominibus** – *worthless men*.

annos natus maior quadraginta: Roscius' age instantly discounts the first category of villainous young man. He is a fully grown adult. As **natus** has no comparative form, **natus maior** is the usual formula for *older than*.

vetus videlicet sicarius: the image of the old assassin clearly does not fit Roscius either as the sarcastic **videlicet** (*obviously*) highlights. Again, a verb *to be* needs to be supplied. The image resembles that painted of Magnus and Capito in other sections of the speech.

in caede versatus: *versor* has the sense of moving around and is often used to mean *occupy* or *dwell among*. Here, its sense is more *occupy oneself with, be engaged in* and should be taken as *practised in*.

hoc ... ne dici quidem audistis: Cicero contrasts his assertions with those of the prosecution. The image of a murderous villain he suggests they have attempted to paint simply does not fit with the evidence they have put forward. **audistis**, a syncopated form of *audivistis*, introduces an accusative and infinitive with **hoc** and **dici** – *you have not even heard this being said*.

luxuries ... aeris alieni magnitudo et indomitae animi cupiditates ... impulerunt: again, Cicero tries to depict his client as subject to vices which haunt the baser Roman and seem particularly characteristic of life in Rome. As a man of the country, Roscius is a model of the long-standing Roman value of *restraint*. **luxuries**, **magnitudo** (modified by **aeris alieni**), and **cupiditates** (modified by **indomitae animi**) are the subjects of the sentence – *Luxuries, the size of his debts and the desires of his untamed spirit drove the man* ... **nimirum** (*no doubt*) again show Cicero's sarcastic tone. **aes alienum** (*another's money*) is the standard formula for *debt*. **luxuries** is an alternative nominative plural for *luxuriae*.

de luxuria purgavit Erucius: Cicero turns the words of Erucius against him. *purgo* is usually used to mean *cleanse* but is used in a legal sense to mean *clear [of a charge]*.

hunc ne in convivio quidem ullo fere interfuisse: Cicero is not as specific as this when he quotes Erucius' argument in Section 52 saying that the Younger Roscius did not attend parties *with his father* and that people rarely invited him to their homes. The sense here is a little more clear-cut although Cicero's use of **ne ... quidem ullo fere** (*hardly any, almost none*) does leave room to manoeuvre.

nihil autem umquam debuit: a flat denial, Cicero's suggestion that debt motivated Roscius is simply not plausible.

ut ipse accusator obiecit, ruri semper habitarit: Cicero's final suggestion, that Roscius may have been driven by *cupiditas* (*lust, passion*) is neatly rebutted using another of Erucius' arguments: Roscius' country life. Erucius must have suggested that the Younger Roscius' dislike of his father (and willingness to murder him) stemmed from resentment that he was given responsibility for tending the land rather than being brought to Rome. Cicero will expand on this at length in the coming sections but, for now, takes the opportunity to highlight the simplicity and lack of temptation in country living. **habitarit** is a syncopated form of the perfect subjunctive *habitaverit*.

quae vita maxime disiuncta a cupiditate: the point is clear, nothing could be further from country living than temptation and desire. Cicero

A Level

takes it further, however, by juxtaposing **cupiditate** with **officio**, a sense of moral duty. **quae** is a connecting relative agreeing with **vita**.

40

quae res igitur tantum istum furorem Sex. Roscio obiecit? Cicero continues his examination of Erucius' arguments to see if there is anything in the case which would point to a motive. **quae** agrees with **res** (*what circumstance*) but **res** is almost redundant in English, a simple *what* sufficing. **obiecit** (*threw out*) could be taken as *presented, brought upon*, although it may be easier to rephrase in English – *What could have driven Sextus Roscius to such fury?* **tantum istum furorem** refers to rage sufficient to murder his own father while **igitur** suggests contrast with the previous section – in the absence of anything in Roscius' life which would predispose him to murder, what could have driven him to such an act?

'patri' inquit 'non placebat.': the use of the dative **patri** suggests that Roscius' father dislikes him, not the other way round. Cicero clearly thinks this argument is weak. It would have to be a particularly intense dislike which the Elder Roscius had for his son to incite a murder. Cicero does not believe that the Elder Roscius' treatment of his son suggests any dislike for him.

patri non placebat? quam ob causam? Rhetorical questions suggesting disbelief at the prospect.

eam quoque iustam et magnam et perspicuam: the feminine refers to **causam** in the previous question – *[for it must have been] a just and great and clear [reason]*.

nam ut illud incredibile est … sic hoc veri simile non est: Cicero finishes the section with two parallel statements, both of which he believes to be extremely unlikely – *for just as it is unbelievable that …, in the same way it is not likely that …* **ut** functions as *just as* introducing the comparison. **illud** refers to the concept of killing one's father. **sic**

pairs with **ut** providing the comparison. **veri simile** (literally *resembling the truth*) can be taken as *likely* or *probable*.

sine plurimis et maximis causis: Cicero accepts that sons do kill fathers but only under the most extreme of circumstances.

odio fuisse parenti filium: accusative and infinitive following **hoc veri simile non est** (*that a son be . . .*). **odio** is predicative dative – *a source of hatred for his father*.

sine causis multis et magnis et necessariis: again, Cicero emphasizes the unlikeliness of this scenario, this time through a tricolon of adjectives. **necesariis** implies there is no possibility but for the father to dislike his son given the circumstances. Consider *compelling* or *cogent*.

41

rursus igitur eodem revertamur et quaeramus: that is to say, looking for evidence that the Younger Roscius was hated by his father.

quae tanta vitia fuerint: indirect question (thus the perfect subjunctive **fuerint**). **quae** agrees with **tanta vitia** which follows – *what great vices . . . .*

in unico filio: Cicero emphasizes that the Younger Roscius is the Elder Roscius' only son to strengthen his argument. There was, in fact, a brother (Cicero mentions him in Section 42) but he had died by this time.

is patri displiceret: emphatic referring to the Younger Roscius – *even he might displease*.

pater igitur amens: this is the only logical conclusion of Cicero's enquiry so far. If the father hated his only son, a man without fault who lived a dutiful life in the country, he must have been mad. As a question, supply the verb *to be* – *Was his father therefore mad . . . ?*

qui odisset eum sine causa quem procrearat: **qui** refers to the elder Roscius – *who hated without cause*. **eum** and **quem** both refer to the Younger Roscius – *the man whom he had fathered*.

at is quidem fuit omnium constantissimus: **is** referring to the Elder Roscius. Cicero's description of him as **constantissimus** is in direct contrast with **amens**. *constantia* (*steadfastness, consistency*) was a prime Roman virtue which differentiated the Romans (as they saw it) from the barbarity of the outside world. A man such as the Elder Roscius, therefore, having demonstrated such a quality could never have been so irrational as to hate his son without reason.

si neque amens pater neque perditus filius fuerit: Cicero closes the argument – if father was not mad and son was not wanton, there is no basis for the prosecution's argument.

neque odi causam patri neque sceleris filio fuisse: accusative and infinitive following **perspicuum profecto est** (*certainly it is clear that …*). **causam** should be taken with both genitives – *there was neither cause for hatred . . . nor for wickedness*. The datives are more easily taken as *on the part of the father . . . on the part of the son*.

42

'nescio' inquit: Cicero is putting words in the prosecution's mouth – we cannot know precisely what arguments they put forward, but they almost certainly did not admit ignorance.

quia antea: *since previously. . . .* Cicero lays out the argument of the prosecution based on the behaviour of the elder Roscius and the differing treatment of the two sons prior to the death of the other.

illum alterum qui mortuus est: *the other who is dead* – i.e. the Younger Roscius' brother.

secum omni tempore volebat esse, hunc in praedia rustica relegarat: the implication is clear – the Elder Roscius displayed a preference for the now deceased brother taking him to Rome, while leaving the Younger Roscius to manage the farms in Ameria. Cicero will present this argument as a nonsense, extolling the virtues of country life, even suggesting that Roscius' father was treating his son well by giving him this wholesome existence. Despite the moral virtue seen in this life by the Romans, Cicero is being slightly disingenuous. Not only was relegation to the country undoubtedly used as a punishment against some Romans, by Cicero's time the opportunities of city life would have held overwhelming appeal to many. **relegarat** is a syncopated form of the pluperfect tense *relegaverat*.

quod Erucio accidebat in mala nugatoriaque accusatione: Cicero's comparison, which he will elucidate shortly, compares Erucius' difficulty in substantiating so weak a charge with Cicero's difficulty, precisely because it is so pathetic, in refuting it.

idem mihi usu venit: as a phrase **usu venit** – *it befalls, it happens upon*.

ille . . . ego: Cicero spells it out for us – **ille** refers to Erucius.

quo modo crimen commenticium confirmaret: *a means by which he can strengthen a fabricated charge*. The indirect question functions as the object of **non inveniebat** which follows.

qua ratione . . . reperire non possum: again, the indirect question forms the object of the main verb – *I am not able to find a basis with which . . . .*

43

quid ais, Eruci? The direct address to Erucius is striking – by drawing him in, Cicero belittles Erucius and his position.

tot praedia tam pulchra, tam fructuosa Sex. Roscius filio suo . . . tradiderat: a display of the Elder Roscius' generosity neatly arranged into a striking tricolon promoted to the beginning of the question for emphasis. How could anyone view such a gift negatively?

A Level

relegationis ac supplici gratia colenda ac tuenda: both genitives **relegationis** and **supplici** follow **gratia** – *for the sake of banishment and punishment* – while **colenda** and **tuenda** (both gerundives) agree with the earlier **praedia** and should be taken as purpose (despite the absence of *ad*) – *to cultivate and oversee*. Both are tautologies for the sake of rhetorical flourish.

quid? Again, addressed to Erucius. These exclamations can be difficult to translate but provide a staccato punch to Cicero's rhythm. Consider: *What's that? What's that you say?*

hoc patres familiae qui liberos habent: the beginning of quite a complex final question in the sentence. **patres familiae** (the subject of the sentence) is a specific legal term for the *head of a household* (often seen in the archaic form *pater familias*). The term denoted the oldest male in a household with responsibility for exercising authority over his family. **hoc** is accusative as part of an indirect statement with **putant** which follows. The sentence can be broken down:

- **patres familiae qui liberos habent** – *heads of households who have children* ....
- **praesertim homines illius ordinis ex municipiis rusticanis** – *especially men of this rank from rural municipalities* ....
- **nonne [hoc] optatissimum sibi putant esse** – *surely they think this [i.e. what follows] to be most agreeable to them* ... (indirect statement which will lead to two further indirect statements).
- **filios suos rei familiari maxime servire** – *that their sons devote themselves most of all to their family estates* ... (first of two indirect statements following **optatissimum ... esse**).
- **et in praediis colendis operae plurimum studique consumere?** – *and that they use up most of their efforts and energy in cultivating the farms?* (a further indirect statement). **colendis** is a gerundive (having undergone gerundival attraction) so **praediis** functions as the object, while **operae** and **studi** are partitive genitives following **plurimum**.

A Level

Cicero's message is clear: the Elder Roscius entrusted his son with the management of the farms as a pursuit which benefitted not only the entire household but also the Younger Roscius. Above all, he did this in a manner which was normal among wealthy families.

44

An amandarat hunc sic: **hunc** referring to the Younger Roscius. **amandarat** implies a malicious sending away or banishment (Cicero uses the noun form *amandatio* later in this section). **amandarat** is a syncopated form of the pluperfect **amandaverat**.

in agro: *in the country* or *in the fields*.

tantum modo: an emphatic form of **tantum** as an adverb meaning *only*. Sometimes seen as a single word *tantummodo*.

aleretur ad villam: *alere* has a sense of supporting as well as feeding or nourishing. The phrasing in the passive *be fed* may (sarcastically) suggest that Roscius was being treated as a domestic animal. **ad villam** (*at the house*) is an alternative to *in villa*.

si constat: impersonal – *it is established*. **hunc** and **praefuisse** which follow form an accusative and infinitive indirect statement.

colendis praediis: gerundival attraction – *of cultivating the farms*. Both are in the dative following **praefuisse**.

patre vivo: ablative absolute – *while his father was still alive*.

frui solitum esse: a continuation of the accusative and infinitive indirect statement started with **si constat** – *he was accustomed to enjoy the use of*. **frui** has a usage which overlaps with **utor** but is more precise in that it suggests benefit or advantage. As *fruor* requires an ablative, **certis fundis** forms the object of the verb.

tamenne haec a te vita ... appellabitur? The resolution of the conditional clause established by **si constat** – *will this life nonetheless*

A Level

still be called by you. . . . **eius** should be taken with **vita** (*this life of his*) referring to Roscius while **rusticana** should be taken with **relegatio** and **amandatio** which follow (which, having almost identical meanings, form a tautology).

quantum distet argumentatio tua: as an adverb, **quantum** has the force of *how much* or *how far* – *how distant your line of argument is . . . .*

ab re ipsa atque a veritate: **re ipsa** (*the matter itself*) should be taken as *the facts of the matter*. Cicero delays **veritate** to the end of the sentence to reinforce that it is his evaluation which constitutes the truth.

quod consuetudine patres faciunt: the relative **quod** is the object of **faciunt** (*that which fathers do . . .*) and is mirrored by **id** in the following clause (*you rebuke this . . .*). Cicero is speaking in general terms – behaviour which Erucius views as evidence of a broken relationship, in Cicero's view, is no different to that of other men of Roscius' class. Cicero repeats the construction two further times:

- **quod benevolentia fit, id . . . criminaris** – *that which was an act of kindness you charge was . . . .*
- **quod honoris causa . . . id eum . . . fecisse dicis** – *that which was done for the sake of honour, you say that he did this . . . .*

There is slight variation each time, introducing the participle **factum** in the second iteration (**id odio factum criminaris** – *you charge that this was done with hatred*) and the use of **causa** (**honoris causa** – *for the sake of honour* – and **supplici causa** – *for the sake of punishment*). The repetition of essentially the same argument but with added variation creates a slight crescendo. Supply *esse* with **factum** to form an indirect statement with the accusative **id. eum** (referring to the Elder Roscius) forms an indirect statement with **fecisse** – *you say that he did this. . . .*

45

neque haec tu non intellegis: the use of the double negative emphasizes the positive – *nor do you not understand these things.*

sed usque eo quid arguas non habes: literally *you do not have anything you might argue to such an extent....* **usque eo ... non** is roughly equivalent to *adeo non* and is usually taken as *so little*. Consider *you have so little to argue*. This naturally leads into the result clause which follows.

tibi ... dicendum putes: a complex and slightly compressed construction. **putes** introduces an indirect statement for which the subject is the impersonal gerundive **dicendum** (supply *esse*) *you think it needs to be spoken*. After the gerundive, the agent is expressed by the dative **tibi** (*by you*). This is more easily expressed in English by removing the passive element. Consider: *you think that you need to speak ....*

contra nos ... contra rerum naturam contraque consuetudinem hominum contraque opiniones omnium: the repeated use of **contra** (anaphora) and the increased scope of Erucius' target (**nos ... rerum naturam ... consuetudinem hominum ... opiniones omnium** – *us ... the nature of things ... the custom of men ... the opinions of all*) emphasizes Cicero's belief that Erucius' argument is made in vain, persuading no one that Roscius' time on the farm was a form of exile imposed by his father.

at enim: although **enim** is usually taken as *for*, it can be used in a similar fashion to *quidem – truly, certainly, indeed*. Some translators imply that Cicero is quoting an imagined prosecution argument – *but, you will say ....*

alterum ... dimittebat, alterum ... patiebatur: if the jurors accept Cicero's preceding argument, that time on the farms is not a punishment, then we also accept that the distinction between the treatment of the two sons is irrelevant.

quaeso, Eruci: *I ask you, Erucius* – a condescending phrase, suggesting that Cicero is pleading with Erucius. Again, his focus on Erucius allows him to belittle the prosecution directly.

ut hoc in bonam partem accipias: indirect command following **quaeso** – *that you receive*. **hoc** refers to what Cicero is about to say. As a phrase,

in bonam partem literally means *in good part* but should be taken to mean *favourably* or *without offence*. In the manner of the modern English 'no offence but …'. Cicero is about to be extremely rude to Erucius.

non enim exprobrandi causa sed commonendi gratia dicam: Cicero takes his time getting up to the personal insult at the beginning of Section 46, allowing him time to get an insincere excuse for his behaviour in first – *for I say this not for the sake of rebuking you, but to remind you.*

46

si tibi fortuna non dedit: *if fortune did not give to you …*, i.e. *if you were not lucky enough, if it was not your lot to …*, paired with **at natura certe dedit** to create contrast.

ut patre certo nascerere: purpose clause following **dedit** – *to be born.* nascor is here followed by the ablative suggesting *born from* or, in more natural English, *born to.* **patre certo** (*to a sure father*) plays on Erucius' low status and the reputation of his mother. Although an experienced and able prosecutor, Erucius was considered of bad character and was of humble background and uncertain parentage. Cicero's willingness to humiliate his opponent in this way is striking.

ex quo intellegere posses: the relative **quo** refers to **patre** – *from whom you might be able to understand …*, the sequence of tense differs from English (*posses* being imperfect) but as Cicero is talking generally about a situation which still stands, a rendering in the present tense seems better suited.

in liberos: *towards his children.*

at natura certe dedit, ut humanitatis non parum haberes: parallel with the constructions above – *but all the same nature certainly gave to you to have …* the genitive **humanitatis** is partitive following **non parum** – *not insufficiently of humanity*, i.e. *a not insufficient level of* *humanity.* Although *humanitas* can refer to education or refinement (similar to *doctrina* which follows), here it stands in addition to it, referring to the quality of being human.

eo accessit: *to this was added* – usually *to approach*, *accedere* can imply increase.

studium doctrinae: *enthusiasm for learning* – as Cicero is about to draw on a tale from the theatre, he needs to credit Erucius with enough knowledge to reckon he will understand the comparison he is about to make.

ut ne a litteris quidem alienus esses: *that you are not indeed a stranger to literature* – result clause using **ne** when paired with **quidem**.

ecquid tandem tibi videtur: the use of **ecquid** strengthens the question which follows – *does he seem to you at all. . . .* **tandem** has a similar role here – *really?*

ut ad fabulas veniamus: a slight aside – literally *to come to plays*. Often taken as *to take an example from the stage* or *to quote a play*.

senex ille Caecilianus: the subject of **videtur**. The adjective **Caecilianus** is formed from the name of the comic playwright Caecilius Statius who was active in the second century BC. None of his plays survive extant (although there are fragments) but we know the titles of many and he was sufficiently popular that his works could be referred to without mentioning him as the author. The work referred to here is likely an adaptation of a play by the Greek comic Menander, known as *Subditivus* (*the counterfeit*). It featured a father with one legitimate and one illegitimate son who were kept apart in the country and the city respectively.

minoris facere Eutychum: an idiomatic phrase – *to care less for. . . .* The infinitive **facere** follows **videtur**. Eutychus is the name of the son raised in the country (**filium rusticum**).

Chaerestratum: the name of the second son kept in the city. Cicero immediately feigns ignorance in an aside (**nam, ut opinor, hoc nomine**

est – *for, I believe, this is his name*) to distance himself from such trivial details.

alterum in urbe secum honoris causa habere: anyone who had seen the play would know that the reverse is true. Again, the infinitive **habere** follows **videtur**.

alterum rus supplici causa relegasse: exactly the argument which Cicero has been refuting since Section 42. A literary trope demonstrating precisely the opposite to Erucius' claim might seem a fitting climax to Cicero's argument, but he will elaborate further in the coming sections. **relegasse** is a syncopated form of **relegavisse** and still follows **videtur**.

47

'quid ad istas ineptias abis?' inquies: Cicero imagines the prosecution response to his line of argument – **ineptias** relates to the mention of Eutychus in the previous section. **quid** should be taken as *why* here. **inquies** is second person future.

quasi vero mihi difficile sit: exactly as the English – *as if it would be difficult for me*. . . . The argument which follows makes plain that Cicero could have called on any number of real-life examples to back up his point.

quamvis multos: literally *however many*, consider *any number*. The masculine **multos** suggests *men*.

ne longius abeam: *so that I do not wander particularly far* – a slight aside, reinforcing the idea that Cicero does not have to look hard to find other men who treat their sons in the same way as Roscius. The comparative **longius** can be taken as *rather far* or *particularly far*.

vel tribules vel vicinos meos: Roman citizens were organized into tribes, originally based on location, which were used as groupings for votes in the tribal assembly. Both **tribules** (*tribesmen*) and **vicinos**

(*neighbours*) are used to further emphasize the ease with which Cicero could look among his associates and find others who would consider rural pursuits positive for their sons.

qui suos liberos . . . agricolas adsiduos esse cupiunt: the relative refers to **tribules** and **vicinos** – *men who desire. . . .* The choice of **adsiduos** is important as, as well as suggesting dedication to a task, it infers a permanent state of affairs. Roman men, in Cicero's mind, have no problem with agriculture being the long-term focus of their sons.

quos plurimi faciunt: idiom – *whom they value most highly.* Consider *their favourites.*

homines notos sumere odiosum est: Cicero avoids naming names with the suggestion that it would be uncouth to do so without their permission. **homines notos** (*well-known men*) is used to contrast with the named character of Eutychus from fiction.

cum et illud incertum sit velintne: *since it is uncertain whether they would want. . . .* **illud** is redundant in English. **cum** goes on to govern **futurus sit** and **intersit** in the following clauses.

nemo vobis magis notus futurus sit: i.e. why would Cicero choose a real-life example, who may we be less well-known, when a literary trope illustrates the point perfectly well.

ad rem nihil intersit utrum . . . an . . . nominem: as an impersonal verb, **intersit** means *make a difference.* When paired with **nihil** – *it makes no difference.* **nominem** should be taken with both **utrum** and **an** – *whether I name . . . or [I name] . . . .*

comicum adulescentem: again, referring to Eutychus (or any other Cicero might care to mention).

aliquem ex agro Veienti: *someone from the district of Veii.* The **ager Veiens** refers to the area around the Etruscan town of Veii. It was eventually conquered under the Roman general Camillus in 396 BC and then occupied by Roman settlers. The direct reference to Veii is

A Level

as a location where a man might find himself occupied by rural work. **agro** could be variously interpreted as *district, territory,* or *countryside.*

haec conficta arbitror esse a poetis: Cicero seeks to further justify his lack of real-life examples arguing that art imitates life – Eutychus would not exist on stage if he did not exist in the families all around us.

ut...nostros mores...expressamque imaginem vitae...videremus: **mores** and **imaginem** are both the object of **videremus**.

in alienis personis: *in the characters of others / in the characters of strangers* – seeing ourselves reflected on the stage is exactly why we go to the theatre. Erucius' argument that a life in the country is punishment is not true whether on stage or in reality.

48

age nunc: a transitional phrase – *come now!*

refer animum sis ad veritatem et considera: the use of the imperatives (**refer, considera**) drives Cicero's listener back to the matter at hand. The use of the singular suggests the intended recipient is Erucius (as will be made clear later). **veritatem** is used to contrast with the discussion of *fabulae* and should be taken as *reality* rather than *truth* – Cicero's concern is real life. **sis** is a contraction of *si vis* and is usually rendered as *if you please.*

non modo in Umbria atque in ea vicinitate: *not only in Umbria and in this region....* **Umbria** is where Roscius' home of Ameria is located. **in ea vicinitate** refers to the area around Rome (including Veii).

sed in his veteribus municipiis: Cicero seeks to broaden his scope. The values the Elder Roscius championed for his son are considered virtues across Italy. The use of **veteribus** adds further strength as it suggests these are traditional Roman values.

quae studia: dependent on **considera** – *consider... which pursuits....*

te intelleges: an accusative and infinitive depending on **dedisse** follows – *you will understand that you have ascribed....* When talking of characteristics, *dare* can mean *impute* or *ascribe*. The datives **vitio** and **culpae** naturally follow – *you have ascribed ... to fault and blame.*

inopia criminum: *through a lack of [real] charges* – **inopia** is a causal ablative.

non modo ... patrum voluntate: *not only by the will of their fathers* – Cicero addresses the argument in greater depth. It is not just that fathers wish this lifestyle for their sons. There is genuine enthusiasm from both parents and sons for a rural mode of living.

permultos et ego novi et ... unus quisque vestrum: *both I and each of you know very many....* **novi** is perfect in form but present in meaning. Although first person, it should also be taken with **unus quisque**.

nisi me fallit animus: a slightly sarcastic aside – *unless my mind deceives me ....*

et ipsi incensi sunt: *are both fired up of their own accord* – **et** is picked up in the following clause by **-que**. The force of **ipsi** is more akin to **ultro** or **sua sponte** here.

quam tu probro et crimini putas esse oportere: *which you think ought to be a source of shame and accusation ...*, both **probo** and **crimini** are predicative datives.

49

quid censes hunc ipsum Sex. Roscium: the phrasing here is awkward when the force of **quid censes** (*what do you think ...?*) is followed by the indirect questions **quo studio** and **qua intellegentia**. There are two possible approaches:

- Revert to a more strictly grammatical reading – *with what enthusiasm, with what understanding do you think this man Sextus*

Roscius to be . . . ? (as if Cicero had written *quo studio, qua intellegentia censes hunc S. Roscium esse . . . ?*).
- Split the question into two – *What do you think about this man Sextus Roscius? With what enthusiasm, with what understanding do you think him to be . . . ?*

The two ablatives of quality (**quo studio, qua intelligentia**) further complicate the matter as they do not translate straightforwardly into English. This could be tackled by:

- supplying a different verb – *with what enthusiasm, with what understanding do you think this man Sextus Roscius is endowed . . . ?*
- taking the two ablatives as if the object of a supplied verb – *what enthusiasm, what understanding do you think he has . . . ?*

ex his propinquis eius, hominibus honestissimis: Cicero takes the opportunity to build up Roscius' credentials by reference to his relations – the superlative **honestissimis** associates him with their positive qualities and is further emphasized by the alliterative **hominibus honestissimis**. The relatives mentioned have likely been called as witnesses in the trial.

non tu in isto artificio accusatorio callidior es: at the same time, Cicero takes the opportunity to take a swipe at Erucius – whatever you may think about Roscius' skills as a farmer, he is a better farmer than you are a prosecutor. **hic** which follows refers to Roscius while **artificio** should be supplied with **suo**.

quoniam ita Chrysogono videtur: Cicero brings us jarringly back to the reality. It is Chrysogonus who is in possession of Roscius' farms. **videtur** with the dative should be taken as *it seems good to . . . .*

et artificium obliviscatur et studium deponat licebit: the impersonal *licet* (*it is allowed*) is regularly followed by subjunctives (although sometimes with *ut*). Thus, *it will be allowed [for him] to both forget . . . and set aside. . . .* The use of *licet* is ironic suggesting that management of the farms was a burden which Roscius will be relieved to be without.

A Level

quod ... miserum et indignum est: **quod** is a connecting relative referring to Roscius' inability to pursue country living.

vitam et famam: Cicero reminds us of the stakes – this is not a case about stolen property, Roscius' life is at risk. The pairing of the two (*life and reputation*) as equally balanced are indicative of the Roman mindset. A life with sullied reputation is no life at all.

propter praediorum bonitatem et multitudinem: Cicero's meaning is plain – Roscius is only on trial because of the number and quality of the farms in his father's possession. The reminder is relatively subtle, assuming his audience accepts his view that the trial is a sham motivated by greed.

ea studiose coluit: a small additional detail which builds Roscius' profile as a man of virtue engaged diligently in simple, meaningful work.

id erit ei maxime fraudi: completion of the conditional clause **si et in hanc...** – *this would be the greatest injustice for him.*

ut parum miseriae sit ... nisi etiam ...: Cicero elaborates on the harm caused to Roscius (*that it would be sufficient misery to have...*) but then instantly takes this further, **nisi etiam** (*unless also...*). To have cultivated one's farms only for someone else to benefit is insult enough, but that the act of taking such good care of them should result in a criminal trial and death is too much to bear. **quod omnino coluit** functions as the subject of the phrase (*the fact that he cultivated them at all*) while **crimini** is a predicative dative after **fuerit** (*should be [considered] a crime*).

50

ne tu, Eruci: Cicero addresses Erucius directly again with a view to further attacking him. **ne** can be used as an interjection meaning *truly, indeed – indeed you, Erucius ....*

A Level

accusator esses ridiculus: the apodosis of the conditional clause which follows (**si illis temporibus natus esses**) in the past – *you would have been a ludicrous prosecutor if....*

cum ab aratro arcessebantur: Cicero looks back to a golden age of the Roman Republic when men of great influence were drawn from the fields to carry out service for the state only to return to them once their task was complete. Cicero draws directly on Atilius in this section, an example which was presumably well-known to his audience, but there are others in the same mould. Perhaps the most obvious is Cincinnatus who is said to have been met by delegates at his farm, called to the office of dictator and then, on completion of his task, to have relinquished the office at the earliest possible opportunity (Livy, *ab urbe condita*, 3.26.7–29.6).

qui praeesse agro colendo flagitium putes: a slightly compressed statement – **qui** refers to Erucius who is the subject of **putes** which follows (*you who think...*), **flagitium** is accusative as part of an indirect statement but the infinitive *esse* should be supplied (*it is a crime ...*) while **praeesse** (which takes a dative) naturally follows with **agro colendo** (the phrase itself subject to gerundival attraction) as its object – *to preside over the cultivation of land.*

illum Atilium ... hominem turpissimum atque inhonestissimum iudicares: the additional relative clauses (**quem sua manu ... qui missi erant ...**) may cause confusion here. The main verb, **iudicares**, is a potential subjunctive with **Atilium** as the object – *you would judge Atilius*. The remaining accusatives are a description of Atilius. The relative clauses need a little unpacking...

- **quem ... qui missi erant convenerunt** – *whom those who had been sent met ...* (**quem** is the object of **convenerunt**).
- **sua manu spargentem semen** – *sowing seed by his own hand ...* (the accusative **spargentem** agrees with **quem** which precedes it).

Atilium: likely refers to Gaius Atilius Regulus Serranus who was consul in 257 BC and 250 BC. At the time of his second election to the consulship, Atilius is said to have been ploughing his fields when a delegation arrived informing him of the outcome of the election.

at hercule: exclamation – *but by Hercules!*

maiores nostri: as a noun **maiores** should be taken as *ancestors, elders, forefathers*.

longe aliter ... existimabant: *they judged very differently* – i.e. from the way in which Erucius portrays those dedicated to cultivation of the land.

de illo et de ceteris talibus viris: **de illo** refers to Atilius while **ceteris talibus viris** is a nod to other well-known examples from Roman history.

ex minima tenuissimaque re publica: Cicero widens the scope of his argument by examining the impact of such men's actions on the Republic. By the time of this speech in 80 BC Rome's influence extended across most of the Mediterranean – clearly the virtues extolled by their forefathers had, in Cicero's mind, been a key factor in Rome's success.

non alienos cupide appetebant: a somewhat paradoxical statement considering the massive growth in Roman territory since the city's foundation. Cicero himself has described the Republic as **maximam** in the previous sentence. It is possible he means us to consider the positive impact of Rome's focus on increasing its own power before looking further outwards or that he views Rome's allies as essentially self-governing (one of the primary factors in the Social War about a decade earlier). The reality is that, since its inception, Rome kept territorial expansion as an almost constant goal.

quibus rebus: i.e. through the behaviours of their forefathers, *virtues* or *behaviours* may be reasonable translations for **rebus** in this context.

rem publicam atque hoc imperium et populi Romani nomen auxerunt: **rem publicam** and **hoc imperium** and **nomen** are all objects

A Level

of **auxerunt**. **populi Romani** modifies **nomen** (*the name of the Roman people*) while the ablatives which precede (**et agris et urbibus et nationibus**) are all instrumental – *with lands and cities and peoples*. The extensive use of polysyndeton gives a weightier tone to this, the climax of the section.

51

eo ... quo conferenda sint: when paired with **quo** the adverb **eo** carries an idiomatic meaning *on the grounds that [they should be compared with ...]*.

ut illud intellegatur: *so that this might be understood* – i.e. that which Cicero is about to expand upon.

cum ... summi viri clarissimique homines ... tamen ... aliquantum operae temporisque consumpserint: a quite complex **cum** clause, the subjects of which are **summi viri** and **clarissimi homines**, dependent on **consumpserint** which follows – *since the greatest and most famous men dedicated....* Rendering both **viri** and **homines** separately is difficult in English and they are perhaps better taken together but the adjectives **summi** and **clarissimi** both have distinct meanings, **summi** referring to their status as men of rank while **clarissimi** refers to renown through moral excellence. The object of the sentence is **aliquantum** which is then modified by the genitives **operae** and **temporis** – *a portion of their effort and time*. **tamen** is concessive – *nevertheless*.

qui ... ad gubernacula rei publicae sedere debebant: *who ought to have sat at the helm of the Republic*. A relative clause describing the **summi viri clarissimique homines** – Cicero is fond of a *ship of state* metaphor (which can be found in other of his speeches) suggesting the wise hand of one guiding the state through rocky and rough seas.

ignosci oportere ei homini: impersonal construction – *it ought to be pardoned to that man....* **oportere** is a present infinitive but should be taken as the main verb.

cum ruri adsiduus semper vixerit: the use of both **adsiduus** (*constant*) and **semper** (*always*) strengthens Cicero's message. Commitment to a country life is not a crime. **adsiduus** is better taken as the adverb, *constantly*.

quod aut patri gratius aut sibi iucundius aut ... honestius: Cicero finishes the section with a tricolon crescendo covering the virtue of country life from all angles: positive to father, to son and to the general good.

52

odium igitur acerrimum patris ... ostenditur: enormously sarcastic – Cicero believes nothing of the sort.

quod hunc ruri esse patiebatur: the subject of **patiebatur** is the Elder Roscius while **hunc** refers to the Younger.

numquid est aliud? 'immo vero': *Is there anything else? 'Certainly.'* Cicero poses the question and then immediately answers it (a technique known as *hypophora*) in the guise of the prosecution (which will then allow him to demolish the presumed argument). This allows him to examine a second aspect of the *probabile ex causa* (see Section 40), the possibility that the Younger Roscius were to be disinherited. **numquid** is a strengthened interrogative. **immo vero** emphasizes the positive response (where one might have expected a negative).

nam istum exheredare in animo habebat: the idiom **in animo habebat** is identical to the English – *he had in mind*. The subject of the verb is the Elder Roscius while **istum** refers to the Younger.

audio; nunc dicis aliquid quod ad rem pertineat: Cicero's use of **audio** is meant sincerely – *I'm listening*. In a case such as this, disinheritance may have been a contributing factor. **pertineat** is a potential subjunctive – *which may relate.* ... **rem** should be taken as *the case, the matter*.

nam illa: *for these.* ... Referencing the arguments which follow, all of which Cicero believes have no bearing on the case.

A Level

'**convivia cum patre non inibat.**' **quippe**: again Cicero puts forward the prosecution's own arguments, allowing him to quickly rebut them. **quippe** shows an immediate acceptance of the argument as natural and reasonable – *of course! certainly!* – and implying an obvious explanation. **inibat** is more easily rendered as *attend*.

qui ne in oppidum quidem nisi perraro veniret: a relative clause showing both cause and characteristic and using the subjunctive. Literally *a man who did not even come into town except rarely*. The causal element is most important here as Cicero is refuting the previous argument – *since he hardly ever even came into town*. Some commentators suggest **oppidum** should be taken as *a town* as the word does not often refer to Rome. However, as the Elder Roscius was usually in Rome, if not in Ameria, and Cicero uses **urbe** shortly afterwards to refer to Rome, it would make much more sense if **oppidum** did indeed refer to the city itself.

'**domum suam istum non fere quisquam vocabat.**' **nec mirum**: a second prosecution argument, immediately countered with **nec mirum** (*no surprise!*). **non fere quisquam** is most easily taken as *hardly anyone*.

qui neque in urbe viveret neque revocaturus esset: parallel in construction to **qui ... veniret** earlier. Again, taking the phrase as causal is most straightforward – *since he neither lived ... nor was going to. ...* **revocaturus** carries the nuance *invite them in return*.

53

tu quoque intellegis: continuing to address Erucius.

illud quod coepimus videamus: jussive subjunctive – *let us. ...* **videamus** needs strengthening a little in English – *consider, examine*. **illud quod** – *that which. ...* Cicero is about to look again at the idea of disinheritance.

'**exheredare pater filium cogitabat.**': again Cicero presents the prosecution's argument with the intention of destroying it.

A Level

mitto quaerere: the sense of **mitto** here is *overlook, omit*. The phrase can be taken as roughly equivalent to *non quaero – I do not ask* . . . .

qui scias: as well as functioning as the relative, **qui** can be the interrogative *how*. It should be taken as such here. Cicero looks to keep the argument simple – why the Elder Roscius would seek to disinherit his son is less important than any proof the prosecution may have that this was even the case. The presumption is that they have none.

tametsi te dicere atque enumerare . . . oportebat: despite his previous statement, Cicero does not miss the opportunity to remind Erucius of his role as a prosecutor. A man doing his job well would include all possible reasons for the disinheritance of the Younger Roscius.

id erat certi accusatoris officium: a clear, personal attack. **certi** should be taken with the more nuanced meaning of *dependable* or *sincere* (which Cicero does not believe Erucius to be). **id erat** is more easily taken as *this would have been . . .* in English.

explicare omnia vitia ac peccata: following **id erat . . . officium** – *to enumerate every vice and fault* . . . .

quibus: instrumental referring to **vitia** and **peccata** – *vice and fault by which* . . . .

ut naturam ipsam vinceret: i.e. the natural inclination of a father to look to his son's advantage. To disinherit a son requires that the Elder Roscius disregard his son's best interests and his own legacy. The first in a series of three purpose clauses – **ut . . . eiceret** and **ut . . . obliviscetur** are parallel in construction, each increasing the emotional anguish which the Elder Roscius would have felt in taking the action which is suggested.

quae . . . accidere potuisse non arbitror: **quae** is accusative as part of an indirect statement following **arbitror** – *things which I do not think could have happened* . . . .

sine magnis huiusce peccatis: Cicero's point is clear – the Younger Roscius must have done something extreme for such a scenario to arise.

A Level

And yet, the prosecution seems to have offered nothing which would suggest such a fundamental rift between him and his father.

54

verum concedo tibi ut ea praetereas quae ... concedis: condescending in tone – Cicero will allow the prosecution to get away with this. But only on the basis that their silence is an admission of failure on their part. The repetition of *concedere* in different forms (polyptoton) is interesting as the nuance is different. When used to refer to himself, **concedo** means *I permit, grant* while **concedis** means *you admit, you concede*, allowing Cicero to emphasize the strengths of their respective positions. **ea** refers to the reasons for the disinheritance of the Younger Roscius.

cum taces: causal – *since you are silent* . . . .

illud: the object of **facere** which follows (itself reliant on **debes**) – *you ought to make clear that fact* . . . .

voluisse exheredare: a description of **illud** which precedes – *the fact that [he] wanted to disinherit [his son]*. A compressed accusative and infinitive indirect statement.

qua re id factum putemus? *by which we might think that this was his intention*. **qua re** (literally *by which matter*) may be taken as *on which grounds*. **factum** (usually *deed, act*), considering Cicero has talked of the desire to disinherit the Younger Roscius, should probably be taken as *intention, design*. A verb *to be* needs to be supplied.

vere nihil potes dicere; finge aliquid saltem: Cicero likely relished the contrast between **vere** (*truly*) and **finge** (*invent*). His faux desperation is, however, reaching fever pitch – so weak is the prosecution's argument that he would rather they made something up than be so obvious about their lack of evidence. **saltem** (*at least!*) reinforces this.

huius miseri fortunis et horum virorum talium dignitati inludere: the inept nature of the prosecution has a more serious side, however, in that they openly mock and disrespect Roscius' misfortune (**huius miseri fortunis**) and the dignity of the jurors (**horum virorum talium dignitati**). **inludere** mirrors the use of **facere** in the phrase **ut ne plane videaris id facere** (*so that you might not seem to do that ... to mock ...*) and takes the dative as object here (**fortunis** and **dignitati**).

exheredare filium voluit. quam ob causam? 'nescio.' exheredavitne? 'non.' quis prohibuit? 'cogitabat.' cogitabat? cui dixit? 'nemini.': a climactic argument between Cicero and the (supposed) statements of the prosecution. Cicero takes the supposition (*he wanted to disinherit his son*) and with a series of short questions (and imagined responses) dismantles it.

- **quam ob causam? 'nescio.'** – *For what reason? I do not know ....*
- **exheredavitne? 'non.'** – *Did he disinherit him? No.*
- **quis prohibuit? 'cogitabat.'** – *Who stopped him? He was thinking about it.*
- **cogitabat? cui dixit? 'nemini.'** – *He was thinking about it? Who did he tell? No one.*

This example of *hypophora* (raising a question and immediately answering it) is extremely potent as the questions and answers are so numerous as to be strikingly convincing while also being framed in the voice of the prosecution. In reality, they did not have the opportunity to respond.

quid est aliud ... abuti ad quaestum atque ad libidinem nisi ... accusare atque id obicere ...: a very complex rhetorical question to finish the section accusing the prosecution of disrespect towards the court, the law and the jurors. It can be broken down as follows:

- **quid est aliud ... abuti** – *what else [does it mean] to abuse ...?* **abutor** (like *utor*) takes objects in the ablative – **iudicio ... legibus ... maiestate ...** (the gravity of these nouns is emphasized by the polysyndeton of **ac**).
- **nisi ... accusare atque id obicere** – *except to accuse ... and to present as evidence [something which] ....*

- **quod ... non modo non possis verum ne ... quidem** – the relative clause is further complicated by the inclusion of the balanced **non modo ... verum ne ... quidem** – *which not only [are you not able] ... but you do not even ....*

55

nemo nostrum est: literally *there is no one of us*, i.e. *there is not one of us ....*

quin sciat: **quin** is negative **qui** (*qui ne*) followed by the subjunctive – *who does not know ....*

tibi inimicitias ... nullas esse: indirect statement following **sciat** – *that there is no hostility for you*. **tibi** is possessive dative, i.e. *that you do not have any....* The tone feels conciliatory, appealing to Erucius' conscience.

qua de causa huic inimicus venias: *why you come here as an enemy for this man* – **huic** refers to Roscius and is perhaps more easily taken as *of this man*. Cicero is turning again to a personal attack against Erucius: he has been corrupted.

sciunt huiusce pecunia te adductum esse: Cicero gradually builds the tension, not directly referring to Chrysogonus and bribery, but presenting the money which has tempted Erucius to become an accessory in the plot against Roscius as the same money which has been stolen from him. **huiusce** is a strengthened form of *huius* and refers to Roscius.

quid ergo est? Exclamatory rhetorical question but compressed and requiring expansion in English – *So, what more is there? What more, therefore, is there to say?*

ita ... te cupidum esse oportebat ut: *you ought to have been desirous ... in such a way that....* Result clause with **ita** as the signal word.

horum existimationem: *the judgement of these men* – i.e. the verdict of the jurors. Erucius must have known that there was a chance the jurors would find against him and taking on such a case was a risk.

legem Remmiam: the details of the Remmian law are unclear, however it seems that under its provisions an accused man could request a hearing of false prosecution before his trial ended. If the accused were acquitted, the jurors would then consider whether the prosecution had knowingly brought a false charge. If found guilty, the prosecutor could be branded on the forehead with a 'K' (*kalumniator, false prosecutor*) and prohibited from bringing further prosecutions. The practice is not widely attested and likely employed rarely but the threat made by Cicero is extremely lightly veiled.

aliquid valere oportere: indirect statement following **putares** – *that you thought [the verdict of these men and the Remmian law] ought....* **valere** follows **oportere** – *to be valid* – while **aliquid** is accusative of respect – *in respect of something*, i.e. *to some extent*. The suggestion is that Erucius has no regard for these things at all.

56

accusatores multos esse in civitate utile est: accusative and infinitive indirect statement – *it is a useful thing that....* Cicero is not attacking prosecutors *per se* but emphasizing the danger of false prosecution. There was no system of public prosecutors in Rome, instead individuals would bring the case to court on behalf of a client.

ut metu contineatur audacia: i.e. so that fear of prosecution will curb the inclinations of individuals.

hoc ita est utile, ut ne . . .: **ita** introduces the result clause which follows – *it is [only] useful in this way....* The force of **ne** complicates the meaning slightly as it suggests a hypothesis – *provided that we are not....*

ne plane inludamur: this is Cicero's major focus here – prosecution is an integral part of the Roman state and the upholding of its legal system but it should be used respectfully and sincerely.

innocens est quispiam: *a certain man is innocent* – a hypothetical scenario which will allow Cicero to explore the role of the prosecutor.

A Level

quispiam is an indefinite pronoun (*a, a certain, a particular*) like *quidam*.

abest a culpa, suspicione... non caret: *he is far from blame but not free from suspicion* – the scenario is very clear: an individual who is innocent but, nevertheless, suspicion falls on him.

tametsi miserum est: *although this is a wretched situation* – **miserum** is neuter and indicates, therefore, that Cicero is no longer talking about the individual previously mentioned.

tamen ei ... possim ... ignoscere: *Nevertheless, I would be able to pardon him* – **ignoscere** takes the dative so **ei** is the object of this verb. **tamen** is concessive.

cum ... habeat: the hypothetical prosecutor is the subject of this verb.

criminose ac suspiciose dicere: both **criminose** and **suspiciose** are adverbs (literally *to say criminally and suspiciously*). More easily rendered as *imputing criminality and suspicion*. The pair could also be taken as a hendiadys – *imputing suspicion of criminal activity*.

ludificari et calumniari sciens non videatur: a pairing of powerful verbs – *to mock and to accuse falsely* – but the key is that the prosecutor appears to be acting in good faith. **sciens** (*knowingly*) reinforces this idea.

quod innocens ... absolvi potest, nocens ... condemnari non potest: Cicero takes a logical approach to the role of the prosecutor: an innocent man, even if accused, can be acquitted but a guilty man cannot be proven so without being accused. Cicero makes significant effort to ensure he cannot be misunderstood – his issue is with prosecution in bad faith, not prosecution itself.

utilius est autem absolvi innocentem quam nocentem causam non dicere: a repetition of the same idea. **utilius est** introduces an indirect statement.

anseribus cibaria publice locantur: *food for the geese is contracted out at public expense* – a flock of geese on the Capitoline Hill was maintained using public funds after the Sack of Rome by Gauls in 390 BC. The Romans were besieged there and when an attempt was made by the Gauls to find a way onto the hill, the geese raised the alarm by honking while the guard dogs remained quiet (Livy, *ab urbe condita*, 5.47.4). **locantur** is a technical term for contracting out tasks which are the responsibility of the state.

at fures internoscere non possunt: the geese and dogs remain the subject of the sentence – *because they are not able to distinguish thieves ...*, i.e. any unexpected presence is likely to rouse them, thief or not. Cicero's suggested comparison between geese and dogs and prosecutors is more than a little flawed – the geese were not employed as lookouts and prosecutors are not paid from the public purse – but it appeals to a sense of decency, positioning Erucius as less useful than the animals employed at Rome.

in eam partem potius peccant quae est cautior: *they err on that side which is the more cautious*, i.e. *they err on the side of caution*. The beasts (as Cicero refers to them) are at least good in their intentions.

quod si luce quoque canes latrent: Cicero takes the comparison even further. One can forgive the dogs barking at individuals during the night, but it would be unreasonable for them to bark all day – in the same way, one can forgive a prosecutor who brings a case based on reasonable evidence, but one who plays the system should not be tolerated.

cum ... salutatum aliqui venerint: the supine, **salutatum**, shows purpose after the verb of motion (**venerint**) – *when people have come to pay their respects. ...* The nuance of the verb is slightly amplified here, meaning something more like *venerate* or *worship*.

eis crura suffringantur: *their legs would be broken* – a clear warning to Erucius to do his job properly. The statement is harsh by modern standards but punishment of animals for failure was not uncommon. Indeed, an annual crucifixion of dogs was made as a sacrifice for their failure to warn against the arrival of the Gauls in 390 BC (Pliny, *Naturalis Historia*, 29.14).

A Level

quod acres sint etiam tum, cum suspicio nulla sit: the comparison (despite its flaws) is clear – prosecution where there is no suspicion should be met with equally harsh punishment.

57

accusatorum ratio: the translation of **ratio** is a little tricky – consider *notion, idea, case*.

alii vestrum anseres sunt: Cicero finally makes the comparison plain – the implied subject is *accusatores*.

tantum modo: a strengthened form of **tantum** as an adverb – *only*.

nocere non possunt: the asyndeton is difficult to reflect in English, considering adding a conjunction – *but are not able . . . .*

alii canes: supply **sunt** from earlier in the sentence.

cibaria vobis praeberi videmus: although prosecutors were not paid by the state, Cicero still uses this as a point of comparison – Erucius undoubtedly expects to receive some sort of reward for his troubles in the same way the dogs and geese are rewarded for their efforts.

in eos impetum facere: i.e. to bring prosecutions against people.

hoc populo gratissimum est: again, Cicero presents the work of the prosecutor as a public service when approached responsibly.

si voletis: an aside – *if you will . . ., if you wish . . . .*

cum verisimile erit: Latin often uses a future (**erit**) where English would use the present – *when it is probable . . . .* Sometimes this is known as a *hidden future*.

aliquem commisisse: indirect statement following **verisimile** – *probably that someone . . . .*

in suspicione latratote: *then bark with suspicion* – **latratote** the future imperative is a relatively rare form, as it refers specifically to a time in the future (difficult to render in English). Compare the maxim *memento mori, remember you will die*. **in suspicione** is more easily taken as *with suspicion / through suspicion*. That Cicero chooses to continue the dog imagery through his choice of verb is striking.

sin autem sic agetis: *but if you behave in this way....* **agetis** is future for an open conditional and should be rendered as present. The phrase itself is a straightforward enough conditional clause (*protasis*) which introduces a complex series of other clauses (both result and conditional) which constitute the remainder of the section. These can be broken down as follows:

- **ut arguatis aliquem ... occidisse**: result clause following **sic**: *in such a way that you accuse....* **arguatis** then introduces an indirect statement with **aliquem occidisse** – *someone of killing....* Clearly not hypothetical, Cicero is talking directly about Roscius.
- **neque dicere possitis**: a second result clause still reliant on **ut** – *and [in such a way that] you are able to say neither ....*
- **ac tantum modo ... latrabitis**: a continuation of the original conditional clause (*protasis*) reliant on **sin** – *and [if] you only bark....* Still, the dog imagery continues. Again, **latrabitis** is future for an open conditional but should be rendered as present.
- **nemo suffringet**: the resolution (*apodosis*) of the conditional clauses – *no one will break ....*
- **sed ... litteram illam ... ad caput adfigent**: a second, alternative, resolution (*apodosis*) of the conditional clause – *but will imprint that letter on your head....* Cicero climaxes with direct references to the punishments for false prosecution (see Section 55).
- **ut postea neminem alium nisi ... accusare possitis**: a final result clause giving the other consequences for his actions – *so that afterwards you will be able to accuse no one else except....* A false prosecutor, branded as such, gained disrepute (*infamia*) and was not able to present cases in court.

crura quidem vobis nemo suffringet: the comparison with the dogs continues – Erucius' fate is in some ways far worse. **vobis** is possessive dative – *the legs to you*, i.e. *your legs*.

si ego hos bene novi: an aside – **hos** refers to the jurors. Cicero's tone suggests he does know them well and what he threatens is a likely outcome.

cui vos usque eo inimici estis: the relative **cui** refers to litteram while **usque eo** function as a single adverb, *so – [that letter] to which you are so hostile* . . . .

ut etiam Kal. omnis oderitis: a further relative clause following **usque eo** – *so hostile that you all.* . . . Cicero is engaging in some rather unpleasant punning. The abbreviation **Kal.** refers to the Kalends, the first day of the Roman month. Because the letters are the same as the first three letters of *Kalumniator* (see Section 55), Cicero suggests that prosecutors hate the very day itself. The pun has further depth in that the Kalends was also the day on which interest penalties were due for those in debt – in the same way as a false prosecutor will pay his debt by having the letters branded on his head.

58–154: For a summary of the rest of the speech, see Introduction pp.15–23.

Vocabulary

An asterisk * denotes a word in OCR's Defined Vocabulary List for AS.

*a, ab (+ *ablative*)	by, from
abeo, abire, abii, abitum	go off, go away
abicio, abicere, abieci, abiectum	I throw away, cast aside, abandon
abs (*alternative form of* ab)	by, from
absolvo, absolvere, absolvi, absolutum	I release, set free, acquit, declare innocent
*absum, abesse, afui	I am absent, am wanting, am lacking
abutor, abuti, abusus sum (+ *ablative*)	I abuse, misuse
*ac	and
accedo, accedere, accessi, accessum	I approach, I am added
*accido, accidere, accidi, accisum	I happen, befall
*accipio, accipere, accepi, acceptum	I receive, accept, take
accusatio, accusationis *f.*	charge, accusation, indictment
accusator, accusatoris *m.*	prosecutor, accuser
accusatorius, -a, -um	of an accuser, pertaining to an accuser
accuso, accusare, accusavi, accusatum	I accuse, indict
*acer, acris, acre	sharp, strict, keen, active, hasty
*ad (+ *accusative*)	to, towards, at
adaugeo, adaugere, adauxi, adauctum	I increase, augment
adduco, adducere, adduxi, adductum	I lead to, bring to
*adeo	so, so much, to such a degree
adeo, adire, adii, aditum	I approach, go to
adfero, adferre, attuli, allatum	I bring forth, offer
adfigo, adfigere, adfixi, adfixum	I fix on, imprint, impress upon
adfinis-e (+ *genitive*)	partaking in, sharing in
adhibeo, adhibere, adhibui, adhibitum	I apply, exert, employ
*adhuc	still, as yet
*adimo, adimere, ademi, ademptum	I take away, take from, deprive of
*adipiscor, adipisci, adeptus sum	I attain, acquire, obtain
adiutor, adiutoris *m.*	helper, assistant
adlego, adlegere, adlegi, adlectum	I choose, recruit, elect
adlevo, adlevare, adlevavi, adlevatum	I lift, lighten, lessen
adsequor, adsequi, adsecutus sum	I reach, attain, acquire

adsiduus, -a, -um	constant, perpetual, busy, occupied, diligent
*adsum, adesse, adfui	I am present, am here
*adulescens, adulescentis *m*.	youth, young man
adulescentia, -ae *f*.	youth
adulescentulus, -i *m*. (*diminutive*)	a very young man
adversarius, -i *m*.	opponent, rival, adversary
*aequus, -a, -um	fair, equitable
aes, aeris *n*.	bronze, money
aetas, aetatis *f*.	age, time of life
affero, afferre, attuli, allatum	I bring to, bring upon
age	(as exclamation) come! come on!
*ager, agri *m*.	land, field, farm, estate
*ago, agere, egi, actum	I do, act, drive, put in motion
agricola, -ae *m*.	farmer
aio (*defective*)	I say, assert, affirm
alienus, -a, -um	another's, of another
aliquanto	somewhat, rather
aliquantum, -i *n*.	some, a considerable amount
*aliquis, aliqua, aliquid	some, someone, something
aliter	otherwise, differently, in another manner
*alius, alia, aliud	other, else
alo, alere, alui, altum	I feed, nourish, support, maintain
*alter, altera, alterum	other, another
alter ... alter ...	one ... the other ...
amandatio, amandationis *f*.	banishment, exile, relegation
amando, amandare, amandavi, amandatum	I send forth, send away, remove
amens, amentis	out of one's mind, mad
amentia, -ae *f*.	madness, mindlessness, insanity
Ameria, -ae *f*.	Ameria (a town in Umbria)
Amerinus, -a, -um	of Ameria
*amicus, -i *m*.	friend
*amitto, amittere, amisi, amissum	I lose, let slip
*amor, amoris *m*.	love, affection
amplitudo, amplitudinis *f*.	dignity, grandeur
amplus, -a, -um	great, large, full, ample
*an	or
*animadverto, animadvertere, animadverti, animadversum	I notice, give attention to, observe

Vocabulary

*animus, -i *m.*	mind, soul
*annus, -i *m.*	year
anser, anseris *m.*	goose
*ante (+ *accusative*)	before
*antea	before, previously
antiquus, -a, -um	old, ancient, (of people or values) old fashioned
aperte	openly, plainly, clearly
appello, appellare, appellavi, appellatum	I call, declare, term, announce
appeto, appetere, appetivi, appetitum	I attack, assault, strive for
appromitto, appromittere	I also promise, promise in addition
*apud (+ *accusative*)	among
aratrum, -i *n.*	plough
arbitror, arbitrari, arbitratus sum	I think, believe, consider
*arcesso, arcessere, arcessivi, arcessitum	I summon, call for
argumentatio, argumentationis *f.*	argument, line of reasoning
argumentum, -i *n.*	argument, evidence, proof
arguo, arguere, argui, argutum	I accuse, charge, attempt to prove that
*arma, -orum *n. pl.*	arms, weapons
artificium, -i *n.*	profession, art, business, skill
*at	but
Atilius, -i *m.*	Atilius (Marcus Atilius Regulus, consul 267 and 256 BC)
atque	and
atrocitas, atrocitatis *f.*	atrocity, severity, enormity
atrox, atrocis	terrible, heinous, atrocious
attentus, -a, -um	attentive, careful
attineo, -ere, attinui, attentum	I concern, I relate to
attribuo, attribuere, attribui, attributum	I bestow upon, impose upon, grant
auctio, auctionis *f.*	auction, public sale
auctoritas, auctoritatis *f.*	power, authority, influence
aucupor, aucupari, aucupatus sum	I lie in wait for, strive for, am on the lookout for
audacia, -ae *f.*	daring, audacity, boldness, temerity
audacter	boldy, courageously
*audax, audacis	bold, audacious, daring
*audeo, audere, ausus sum	I dare, I venture, I risk
*audio, audire, audivi, auditum	I hear, listen to
*aufero, auferre, abstuli, ablatum	I carry off, take away, steal

*augeo, augere, auxi, auctum	I augment, strengthen, increase, enlarge
*aut	or
aut ... aut ...	either ... or ...
*autem	but, however
*auxilium, -i *n.*	help, aid, support
Baliaricus, -i *m.*	Baliaricus (a cognomen)
balneae, -arum *f. pl.*	baths
*bellum, -i *n.*	war
*bene	well
benevolentia, -ae *f.*	kindness, benevolence
bestia, -ae *f.*	beast, animal
*bona, -orum *n. pl.*	goods, possessions, property
bonitas, bonitatis *f.*	excellence, goodness
*bonus, -a, -um	good
*brevis, -e	short, brief
C. (*abbreviation*)	Gaius
Caecilia, -ae *f.*	Caecilia (a name)
Caecilianus, -a, -um	Caecilian, of Caecilius
*caedes, caedis *f.*	murder, slaughter, assassination
calamitas, calamitatis *f.*	damage, harm, misfortune, disaster
callidus, -a, -um	clever, skillful, practised, experienced
calumnior, calumniari, calumniatus sum	I make false statements, blame unjustly, contrive tricks, intrigue
*canis, canis *c.*	dog
*capio, capere, cepi, captum	I capture, seize
Capito, Capitonis *m.*	Capito (a name)
Capitolium, -i *n.*	the Capitol, the Capitol Hill
*caput, capitis *n.*	head, life
careo, carere, carui, caritum (+ *ablative*)	I am without, am deprived of, am destitute of
*castra, -orum *n. pl.*	camp, military camp
*causa (+ *genitive*)	for the sake of
*causa, -ae *f.*	case, cause, reason
cautus, -a, -um	careful, cautious
*caveo, cavere, cavi, cautum	I am on my guard, take care
*cena, -ae *f.*	dinner, meal
censeo, censere, censui, censum	I resolve, determine, am of the opinion

certe	certainly, undoubtedly, assuredly
certo	with certainty, for sure
***certus, -a, -um**	certain, resolved, determined, (of objects) settled, fixed, particular, specified
cervix, cervicis *f.*	neck
ceterus, -a, -um	other, rest
Chaerestratus, -i *m.*	Chaerestratus (a name)
Chrysogonus, -i *m.*	Chrysogonus (freedman of Sulla)
cibaria, -orum *n. pl.*	food, corn, feed
cisium, -i *n.*	light carriage (with two wheels)
***civitas, civitatis** *f.*	state, body of citizens
***clam**	in secret, secretly, privately, covertly
***clamo, clamare, clamavi, clamatum**	I cry out, shout out
***clarus, -a, -um**	celebrated, renowned, illustrious
cliens, clientis *m.*	client, dependant
coeo, coire, coii, coitum	I come together, (of partnerships) form, enter into
***coepi, coepisse, coeptum** (*defective – perfect forms only*)	I began
***cogito, cogitare, cogitavi, cogitatus**	I think, consider, reflect upon
cognatus, -i *m.*	relation, relative
cognomen, cognominis *n.*	surname, family name
***cognosco, cognoscere, cognovi, cognitum**	I get to know, recognize, acknowledge
***cogo, cogere, coegi, coactum**	I urge, force, compel
***colo, colere, colui, cultum**	I cultivate, care for
comicus, -a, -um	comic, of comedy, represented in comedy
commemoro, commemorare, commemoravi, commemoratum	I call to mind, recall, remind
commenticius, -a, -um	devised, fabricated
***committo, committere, commisi, commissum**	I put together, begin, commit
commoditas, commoditatis *f.*	fitness, appropriateness, advantage
commodum, -i *n.*	goods, possessions, property
commodus, -a, -um	convenient, suitable, appropriate
commoneo, commonere, commonui, commonitum	I remind, impress upon, put in mind
***comparo, comparare, comparavi, comparatum**	I make ready, arrange, procure

complecto, complectĕre, complecti, complexum	I embrace, include, encompass
concedo, concedere, concessi, concessum	I grant, concede, allow, consign
*condemno, condemnare, condemnavi, condemnatum	I condemn, convict, judge guilty
condicio, condicionis *f.*	condition, terms, proposition
*confero, conferre, contuli, collatum	I bring together, carry together, compare, make a comparison
confingo, confindere, confinxi, confictum	I invent, devise
confirmo, confirmare, confirmavi, confirmatum	I make strong, stengthen, confirm, give assurance of
conflo, conflare, conflavi, conflatum	I blow up, kindle, bring about
confugio, confugere, confugi	I flee, take refuge
coniungo, coniungere, coniunxi, coniunctum	I join, connect, bind
*conor, conari, conatus sum	I try, endeavour, undertake, attempt
conqueror, conqueri, conquestus sum	I complain, lament, make a complaint
conservo, conservare, conservavi, conservatum	I maintain, keep safe, preserve
considero, considerare, consideravi, consideratum	I consider, inspect, examine, reflect on
*consilium, -i *n.*	counsel, deliberative body, court
constans, constantis	unchangeable, constant, stable
*constituo, constituere, constitui, constitutum	I declare, decree
consto, constare, constiti, constatum	(of facts) I am established, am settled (often impersonal)
consuesco, consuescere, consuevi, consuetum	I am accustomed, tend to
consuetudo, consuetudinis *f.*	custom, tradition, habit, ease, familiarity, conversation
*consul, consulis *m.*	consul (highest magistrates of the Republic)
consulto	deliberately, on purpose
*consumo, consumere, consumpsi, consumptum	I use up, eat up, devour
contentus, -a, -um	happy, satisfied, content
contineo, continere, continui, contentum	I limit, restrain, repress
*contra	in turn, in reply, on the other hand
convenio, convenire, conveni, conventum	I assemble, convene, meet, visit
convivium, -i *n.*	banquet, feast

copiosus, -a, -um	rich, copious, plentiful
Cornelius, -i *m.*	Cornelius (a member of the gens Cornelia)
***corpus, corporis** *n.*	body, corpse
corrumpo, corrumpere, corrapi, corruptum	I corrupt, ruin, destroy
cotidianus, -a, -um	daily, everyday
***cotidie**	daily, everyday
***credo, credere, credidi, creditum**	I believe, I trust
***crimen, criminis** *n.*	charge, accusation
criminor, criminari, criminatus sum	I charge, denounce
criminosus, -a, -um	reproachful, accusatory
***crudelis, -e**	cruel, savage
cruor, cruoris *m.*	blood, gore
crus, cruris *n.*	leg, shin
culleus, -i *m.*	leather bag, leather sack
***culpa, -ae** *f.*	guilt, blame
***cum** (+ *ablative*)	with
***cum** (+ *subjunctive*)	when, since
cumulo, cumulare, cumulavi, cumulatum	I heap up, pile up, increase, crown
cumulus, -i *m.*	heap, crown
cupide	eagerly, graspingly, greedily
cupiditas, cupiditatis *f.*	desire, passion
***cupidus, -a, -um**	desirous, eager
***cupio, cupere, cupivi, cupitum**	I desire, wish, long for
***custodio, custodire, custodivi, custoditum**	I guard, protect, defend
damnatio, damnationis *f.*	condemnation, conviction
damno, damnare, damnavi, damnatum	I condemn, convict, judge guilty
***de** (+ *ablative*)	from, down from, about
***debeo, debere, debui, debitum**	I ought, should
decem	ten
decretum, -i *n.*	a decree
decurio, decurionis *m.*	member of a municipal senate, decurio
dedecus, dedecoris *n.*	shame, disgrace
dedo, dedere, dedidi, deditum	I give away, surrender, give up, give over, devote
***defendo, defendere, defensi, defensum**	I defend, guard, protect
defero, deferre, detuli, delatum	I bring away, (with **nomen**) indict, accuse

deficio, deficere, defeci, defectum	I fail in, am discouraged
defungor, defungi, defunctus sum (+ *ablative*)	I have done with, acquit myself of
*deinde	then, next, second
*deleo, delere, delevi, deletum	I erase, destroy, blot out
deliberatus, -a, -um	resolved upon, determined, certain
deligo, deligere, delegi, delectum	I choose, select
deludo, deludere, delusi, delusum	I deceive, mock, make fun of
demonstro, demonstrare, demonstravi, demonstratum	I point out, indicate, show
*denique	finally, lastly
depono, deponere, deposui, depositum	I lay aside, resign, give up
desero, deserere, deserui, desertum	I foresake, abandon
*despero, desperare, desperavi, desperatum	I despair, give up
despicio, despicere, despexi, despectum	I look away, am inattentive, am off my guard
desum, deesse, defui	I lack, am missing, am wanting
*deus, -i *m.*	god
*dico, dicere, dixi, dictum	I speak, say
*dies, diei *m.*	day
differo, differre, distuli, dilatum	I defer, put off, delay
*difficilis, -e	hard, difficult, troublesome
*dignitas, dignitatis *f.*	dignity, merit, worth, greatness
*dignus, -a, -um (+ *ablative*)	worthy of, suitable for, appropriate
diligentia, -ae *f.*	diligence, faithfulness, care
diluculum, -i *n.*	daybreak, dawn
diluo, diluere, dilui, dilutum	I wash away, do away with, remove, weaken
*dimitto, dimittere, dimisi, dimissum	I send away, dismiss
diripio, diripere, diripui, direptum	I plunder, pillage, ravage
*discedo, discedere, discessi, discessum	I leave, depart
discrimen, discriminis *n.*	decisive moment, crisis, danger
disiungo, disiungere, disiunxi, disiunctum	I divide, separate, remove
displiceo, displicere, displicui, displicitum	I displease, dissatisfy
dissolutus, -a, -um	lax, negligent, inattentive, dissolute
distentus, -a, -um	engaged, busied, occupied

disto, distare (*defective*)	I stand apart, am separate, am distant, am different
*****diu**	for a long time, long while
diutius (*comparative:* **diu**)	longer
divinus, -a, -um	divine, godly
*****do, dare, dedi, datum**	I give, give over, hand over, impute
*****doceo, docere, docui, doctum**	I teach, inform, tell
doctrina, -ae *f.*	learning, erudition
domesticus, -a, -um	domestic, private
dominor, dominari, dominatus sum	I have dominion, rule, govern
*****dominus, -i** *m.*	master, owner
*****domus, -us** *f.*	house, home
donatio, donationis *f.*	donation, giving, presenting, largess
dono, donare, donavi, donatum	I give (as a present)
duo, duae, duo	two
*****e, ex** (+ *ablative*)	from, out of
ecquid	... at all? ... perchance? (strengthens a question)
effingo, effingere, effinxi, effictum	I fashion, portray, represent, express
effundo, effundere, effudi, effusum	I pour out, lavish, squander, waste
effusus, -a, -um	profuse, lavish, extravagant
egens, egentis	needy, poor
egestas, egestatis *f.*	extreme poverty, penury, want, need
*****ego, mei**	I
eicio, eicere, eieci, eiectum	I throw out, expel, banish, drive out into exile
*****emo, emere, emi, emptum**	I buy, purchase
emptio, emptionis *f.*	buying, purchase
*****enim**	for, truly, certainly
enumero, enumerare, enumeravi, enumeratum	I enumerate, recount, relate
*****eo**	(of measure) so much, to such an extent, (of location) there
*****ergo**	therefore, accordingly
eripio, eripere, eripui, ereptum	I tear out, snatch away
Erucius, -i *m.*	Erucius (the prosecutor)
*****et**	and
et ... et ...	both ... and ...
etenim	for, for truly, for indeed, certainly

*etiam	even, also
Eutychus, -i *m.*	Eutychus (a name)
evello, evellere, evelli, evolsum	I pluck out, tear away
*exemplum, -i *n.*	example, model
exheredo, exheredare, exheredavi, exheredatum	I disinherit, deprive an heir
eximo, eximere, exemi, exemptum	I take away, remove
existimatio, existimationis *f.*	judgement, reputation, good name
existimo, existimare, existimavi, existimatum	I reckon, think, suppose
exopto, exoptare, exoptavi, exoptatum	I long for, wish for, desire
expello, expellere, expuli, expulsum	I drive out, drive away
explico, explicare, explicavi, explicatum	I disentangle, unfold, set forth
expono, exponere, exposui, expositum	I put forth, relate, explain
exprimo, exprimere, expressi, expressum	I represent, model, portray
exprobro, exprobrare, exprobravi, exprobratum	I reproach, blame, censure, find fault
exsisto, exsistere, exstiti, exstitum	I am visible, exist, arise
exspectatio, exspectationis *f.*	expectation
exsulto, exsultare, exsultavi, exsultatum	I rejoice in, revel in
extraho, extrahere, extraxi, extractum	I pull out, withdraw, extract
exturbo, exturbare, exturbavi, exturbatum	I drive out, drive away
fabula, -ae *f.*	story, play
*facilis, -e	easy
*facinus, facinoris *n.*	deed, crime
*facio, facere, feci, factum	I do, make, (of actions) behave, act
factum, -i *n.*	deed, act
*fallo, fallere, fefelli, falsum	I deceive, trick, cheat
*fama, -ae *f.*	fame, character, reputation
*familia, -ae *f.*	family, household
familiaris, familiaris *m.*	friend, intimate acquaintance
familiaris, -e	family, familial, domestic, of a household
Fannius, -i *m.*	Fannius (praetor presiding over the court)
fateor, fateri, fassus sum	I confess, avow, grant, acknowledge
fautor, fautoris *m.*	favourer, promoter, supporter
felicitas, felicitatis *f.*	luck, good fortune, happiness
*felix, felicis	lucky, fortunate, happy

*fere	nearly, almost, (with negative) scarcely, hardly
*fero, ferre, tuli, latum	I carry, bear, endure
*ferrum, -i *n.*	iron, sword
ferus, -a, -um	wild, untamed, savage
*fides, fidei *f.*	good faith, integrity, protection, support
*filia, -ae *f.*	daughter
*filius, -i *m.*	son
fingo, fingere, finxi, fictum	(in speech or thought) I imagine, suppose, judge
*fio, fieri, factus sum	I become, result, arise
flagitiosus, -a, -um	shameful, disgraceful
flagitium, -i *n.*	outrage, shameful act, disgrace, crime
fletus, -us *m.*	weeping, wailing, lamentation
floreo, florere, florui	I flourish, am prosperous, am eminent
focus, -i *m.*	hearth, fireplace
fore (*future infinitive of* sum)	would be, to be going to be
fore ut	to be on the point of, to reach the point that
formido, formidinis *f.*	fearfulness, terror, awe
forsitan	perhaps
*fortis, -e	strong, brave, mighty
*fortuna, -ae *f.*	fortune, fate, luck
*forum, -i *n.*	forum, market-place
fraus, fraudis *f.*	fraud, deception, crime
frequens, frequentis	often, much, regular
fretus, -a, -um (+ *ablative*)	relying on
fructuosus, -a, -um	productive, bountiful, fruitful
fruor, frui, fructus sum (+ *ablative*)	I enjoy, delight in, enjoy the use of
*fugio, fugere, fugi, fugitum	I flee, run away
fundus, -i *m.*	land, farm, estate
funus, funeris *n.*	funeral, burial, funeral rites
fur, furis *m.*	thief
*furor, furoris *m.*	rage, madness, passion, fury
furtum, -i *n.*	theft, robbery
gemitus, -us *m.*	groaning, lamentation, complaint
*genus, generis *n.*	birth, family, race
*gero, gerere, gessi, gestum	I do, act, bring about, arrange

gladiator, gladiatoris *m.*	gladiator, fighter, cutthroat
Glaucia, -ae *m.*	Glaucia (a family name)
***gratia** (+ *genitive*)	on account of, for the sake of
***gratia, -ae** *f.*	favour, esteem, friendship
gratiosus, -a, -um	popular, full of favour, beloved
gratus, -a, -um	pleasing, agreeable
gravitas, gravitatis *f.*	weight, heaviness, seriousness, severity
graviter	strongly, forcefully, impressively
gubernaculum, -i *n.*	helm, rudder
guberno, gubernare, gubernavi, gubernatum	I steer, govern, direct
***habeo, habere, habui, habitum**	I hold, have, consider
***habito, habitare, habitavi, habitatum**	I live in, inhabit, dwell in
hercule (*exclamation*)	by Hercules!
hercules (*exclamation*)	by Hercules!
***hic**	here
***hic, haec, hoc**	this
hice, haece, hoce	strengthened form of hic, haec, hoc
***hodie**	today, at present, at this time
***homo, hominis** *c.*	man, person
honestas, honestatis *f.*	honour, repute, reputation, respectability
honestus, -a, -um	honest, worthy, decent
honos, honoris *m.* (*alternative:* **honor**)	honour, respect, dignity
***hora, -ae** *f.*	hour
horreo, horrere, horrui	I shake, tremble, quake
***hospes, hospitis** *m.*	guest, host, connection, friend (bound by ties of hospitality)
hospitium, -i *n.*	hospitality, tie, relationship
***huc**	to this, to this point
humanitas, humanitatis *f.*	humanity, human nature, human feeling
humanus, -a, -um	human, of man
iacto, iactare, iactavi, iactatum	I throw, (*with* **se**) I boast, brag, make a display
***iam**	now, already
ibidem	on the spot, immediately, in this very place
***idem, eadem, idem**	the same
***idoneus, -a, -um**	apt, suitable, capable

*igitur	therefore, accordingly
*ignoro, ignorare, ignoravi, ignoratum	I do not know, am ignorant of
ignosco, ignoscere, ignovi, ignotum	I pardon, forgive
ignotus, -a, -um	unknown, obscure, without repute
*ille, illa, illud	that, he, she, it
imago, imaginem *f.*	image, representation, likeness
immanis, -e	monstrous, immense, savage, wild
immo	indeed, assuredly, certainly, (*with negative*) by no means, on the contrary
immortalis, -e	immortal, undying
impedimentum, -i *n.*	impediment, obstacle, hindrance
*impedio, impedire, impedivi, impeditum	I hinder, hamper, shackle
impello, impellere, impuli, impulsum	I drive on, urge on
impendeo, -ere	I hang over, threaten
*imperium, -i *n.*	power, empire, dominion
impertio, impertire, impertivi, impertitum	I bestow, share, impart, show
*impetus, -us *m.*	attack, assault
imploro, implorare, imploravi, imploratum	invoke, implore, beseech
impono, imponere, imposui, impositum	I place on, set upon, impose upon
improbus, -a, -um	bad, wicked, base, shameless
imprudens, imprudentis	unaware, unsuspecting, without knowledge
*in (+ *ablative*)	in, on
*in (+ *accusative*)	into, onto, against
incautus, -a, -um	uncautious, unsuspicious, imprudent
*incendo, incendere, incendi, incensum	I inflame, kindle, rouse, excite
incertus, -a, -um	uncertain, doubtful
incolumis, -e	safe, sound, whole
incredibilis, -e	incredible, unbelievable, extraordinary
indignus, -a, -um	unworthy, shameful, intolerable
indomitus, -a, -um	untamed, unrestrained
induco, inducere, induxi, inductum	I lead on, seduce, incite, mislead
industria, -ae *f.*	industry, diligence, hard work, effort
ineo, inire, inii, initum	I go into, I enter
ineptia, -ae *f.*	folly, absurdity
ineptus, -a, -um	senseless, silly, absurd, childish
infestus, -a, -um	hostile, troublesome, dangerous

infirmitas, infirmitatis *f.*	weakness, feebleness
infirmo, infirmare, infirmavi, infirmatum	I weaken, enfeeble, refute, disprove
*ingenium, -i *n.*	quality, character, intelligence, capacity
inhonestus, -a, -um	dishonourable, disgraceful, shameful
inimicitia, -ae *f.*	enmity, hostility
*inimicus, -i *m.*	enemy
*initium, -i *n.*	beginning, start, commencement
iniuria (*as adverb*)	unjustly, in an unjust manner
inludo, inludere, inlusi, inlusum (+ *dative*)	I mock, ridicule
innocens, innocentis	innocent, blameless
*inopia, -ae *f.*	poverty, lack, insecurity, helplessness
inops, inopis	helpless, weak, destitute, wretched
inoratus, -a, -um	not pleaded, not heard, unspoken
*inquam (*defective*)	I say
insero, inserere, insevi, insitum	I implant, sow
*insidiae, -arum *f. pl.*	plot, trap
insolens, insolentis	arrogant, excessive, insolent
insto, instare, institi, instatum	I draw near, approach, threaten
insuo, insuere, insui, insutum	I sew in, stitch in
intellegentia, -ae *f.*	discernment, shrewdness, understanding, intelligence
*intellego, intellegere, intellexi, intellectum	I understand, realize, feel, recognize
intendo, intendere, intendi, intentum	I stretch out, extend, threaten
*inter (+ *accusative*)	among, between
*interea	meanwhile
internosco, internoscere, internovi, internotum	I distinguish, discern, tell apart
intersum, interesse, interfui	I am present at, take part in, attend
intervallum, -i *n.*	space, interval, pause
invado, invadere, invasi, invasum	I fall upon, seize, take possession of
*invenio, invenire, inveni, inventum	I find, come across, discover
*ipse, ipsa, ipsum	self, himself, herself, itself
*is, ea, id	this, that, he, she, it
iste, ista, istud	this, that, he, she
*ita	so, thus, in this way
*itaque	and so, therefore
*iter, itineris *n.*	journey, path, road

iucundus, -a, -um	delightful, pleasant
*****iudex, iudicis** *c.*	judge, juror
iudicium, -i *n.*	trial, court, judgement
iudico, iudicare, iudicavi, iudicatum	I judge, pass judgement, decide
iugulo, iugulare, iugulavi, iugulatum	I kill, slay, murder, cut the throat of
iuro, iurare, iuravi, iuratum	I swear
ius iurandum *n.*	(the swearing of) an oath
ius, iuris *n.*	right, justice, law
iusta, -orum *n. pl.*	due ceremonies, formalities
*****iustus, -a, -um**	just, upright, righteous
Kal. (*abbreviation:* **Kalendae, Kalendarum,** *f. pl.*)	Calends, first day of the month
L. (*abbreviation*)	Lucius
*****laedo, laedere, laesi, laesum**	I hurt, wound, injure
lanista, -ae *m.*	trainer of gladiators, tutor, coach
largus, -a, -um	abundant, copious, plentiful
latro, latrare, latravi, latratum	I bark
latro, latronis *m.*	robber, bandit
*****laudo, laudare, laudavi, laudatum**	I praise, celebrate, commend
*****laus, laudis** *f.*	praise, fame, glory
*****legatus, -i** *m.*	ambassador, legate
*****lentus, -a, -um**	slow, sluggish, (of personalities) indifferent, unconcerned
*****levis, -e**	light, trifling, trivial, unimportant
levo, levare, levavi, levatum	I lighten, relieve, ease
*****lex, legis** *f.*	law
libenter	willingly, gladly
*****liber, libera, liberum**	free, unrestrained
*****liberi, -orum** *m. pl.*	children
*****libertas, libertatis** *f.*	liberty, freedom
libertinus, -i *m.*	freedman, former slave
*****libertus, -i** *m.*	freedman, former slave
libido, libidinis *f.*	lust, pleasure, desire
licet (*as conjunction in opposition to main clause*)	even if, even though, despite
*****licet, licere, licuit, licitum** (*impersonal*)	It is lawful, allowed, permitted
*****littera, -ae** *f.*	letter
litterae, -arum *f. pl.*	literature

loco, locare, locavi, locatum	I contract out
longe	far, by far, long
*****longus, -a, -um**	long, sustained
*****loquor, loqui, locutus sum**	I speak, say, talk
luctus, -us *m.*	sorrow, mourning, grief
ludificor, ludificari, ludificatus sum	I mock, deceive, thwart, frustrate
*****lux, lucis** *f.*	light, daytime, day
luxuria, -ae *f.*	luxury, extravagance, excess
luxuries (*acc:* **luxuriem**)	luxury, excess, extravagance
M. (*abbreviation*)	Marcus
*****magis**	more, rather
*****magister, magistri** *m.*	teacher, master
magnitudo, magnitudinis *f.*	greatness, size, magnitude
*****magnus, -a, -um**	big, great
Magnus, -i *m.*	Magnus (a name)
maiestas, maiestatis *f.*	greatness, grandeur, dignity, majesty
maior, maius	bigger, greater (*comparative of* **magnus**)
maiores, maiorum *m. pl.*	elders, ancestors, forefathers
maleficium, -i *n.*	wickedness, offence, crime
Mallius, -i *m.*	Mallius (a name)
*****malo, malle, malui**	I prefer, would rather
*****malus, -a, -um**	bad, evil, wicked
manceps, mancipis *m.*	buyer, purchaser (at auction)
manifestus, -a, -um	open, clear, obvious, visible
*****manus, -us** *f.*	hand
maximus, -a, -um (*superlative of* **magnus**)	very great, greatest
medium, -i *n.*	middle
mentio, mentionis *f.*	mention, naming
mereor, mereri, meritus sum	I deserve, I merit
Metelli, -orum *m. pl.*	the Metelli (prominent Roman family)
metuo, metuere, metui, metutum	I fear, am afraid of
*****metus, -us** *m.*	fear, dread, anxiety
*****meus, -a, -um**	my, mine
mille	a thousand
mille passuum (*pl.* **milia passuum**)	a mile (a thousand paces)
minae, -arum *f. pl.*	threats, menaces
minimus, -a, -um (*superlative adjective from* **parvus**)	smallest, least

Vocabulary

minor, minus (*comparative adjective from* **parvus**)	less
minus (*comparative adverb from* **parvus**)	less
mirus, -a, -um	surprising, astonishing
***miser, misera, miserum**	miserable, wretched
miseria, -ae *f.*	wretchedness, unhappiness, misery
***mitto, mittere, misi, missum**	I send, despatch, pass over
***modus, -i** *m.*	way, manner, method
molior, moliri, molitus sum	I try, endeavour, undertake, attempt
mordeo, mordere, momordi, morsum	I bite
***morior, mori, mortuus sum**	I die
***mors, mortis** *f.*	death
mortalis, -e	mortal
mortuus, -a, -um	dead
***mos, moris** *m.*	habit, manner, custom
***mulier, mulieris** *f.*	woman
***multitudo, multitudinis** *f.*	crowd, throng
***multus, -a, -um**	much, (*in plural*) many
municeps, municipis *c.*	citizen, townsman
municipium, -i *n.*	municipium, free town of Roman citizens

***nam**	for, since
***nascor, nasci, natus sum** (+ *ablative*)	I am born (of)
natio, nationis *f.*	nation, people, state
***natura, -ae** *f.*	nature, character, inclination
natus, -a, -um	born, aged
***ne** (+ *subjunctive*)	that not, so that not, in order not
***ne** (*as suffix*)	particle which forms a question
ne (*as interjection*)	truly, really, indeed
ne ... quidem	not even, not indeed
***nec**	and not, no
necessarius, -a, -um	necessary, requisite, cogent, compelling
***necesse** (*indeclinable*)	necessary, inevitable
nefarius, -a, -um	heinous, criminal, wicked, unholy
***neglego, neglegere, neglexi, neglectum**	I ignore, disregard, neglect
***negotium, -i** *n.*	business, occupation, difficulty, trouble
***nemo** (*accusative:* **neminem**) *m.* or *f.*	no one, nobody
Nepos, Nepotis *m.*	Nepos (a name)
nequam (*indeclinable*)	worthless, good for nothing

*neque	and not
neque ... neque ...	neither ... nor ...
*nescio, nescire, nescivi	I do not know, am ignorant of
*nihil (*indeclinable*)	nothing
nimirum	doubtless, certainly, truly, surely
*nisi	if not, unless, except
*nobilis, -e	noble, eminent
nobilitas, nobilitatis *f.*	nobility, noble origin, high birth, (of objects) splendid
nocens, nocentis	guilty, culpable, criminal
*noceo, nocere, nocui, nocitum	I harm, injure
noctu	by night, at night
nocturnus, -a, -um	of night, nocturnal
*nomen, nominis *n.*	name
nominatim	by name, in detail
nomino, nominare, nominavi, nominatum	I name, mention by name
*non	not
non modo ...	not only
*nondum	not yet
*nonne	surely?
*nos, nostrum / nostri	we
*noster, nostra, nostrum	our
*notus, -a, -um	known, eminent, familiar
*novi, novisse, notum (*perfect form, present meaning*)	I know
*novus, -a, -um	new, novel, (*negative*) strange, unheard of
*nox, noctis *f.*	night
nudus, -a, -um	bare, naked
nugatorius, -a, -um	trifling, worthless, futile
*nullus, -a, -um	no, not any, none
numero, numerare, numeravi, numeratum	I count, regard, consider
*numerus, -i *m.*	number, body, quantity
nummus, nummum	coin, sestertius
numquid	anything, anything further
*nunc	now, at this time
*nuntio, nuntiare, nuntiavi, nuntiatum	I announce, declare, report, bring news
*nuntius, -i *m.*	messenger, news
nuper	newly, recently, lately

*ob (+ *accusative*)	on account of, for, by reason of
obicio, obicere, obieci, obiectum	I use as a defence, present, offer, slander, reproach, expose
*obliviscor, oblivisci, oblitus sum	I forget
obscurus, -a, -um	dark, obscure
obsecro, obsecrare, obsecravi, obsecratum	I implore, beseech
observo, observare, observavi, observatum	I watch, observe
*obsideo, obsidere, obsedi, obsessum	I besiege, blockade
obsto, obstare, obstiti	I stand in the way, obstruct
obtineo, obtinere, obtinui, obtentum	I hold, have, keep possession of
*occido, occidere, occidi, occisum	I kill, slay, put to death
occupatio, occupationis *f*.	employment, occupation
*oculus, -i *m*.	eye, (*figurative*) sight
odiosus, -a, -um	hateful, odious, unpleasant, offensive
*odium, -i *n*.	hate, hatred, animosity, enmity
*offero, offerre, obtuli, oblatum	I offer, bring before, inflict upon
officio, officere, offeci, offectum	I come in the way of, hinder
*officium, -i *n*.	duty, service, obligation
*omnino	altogether, wholly, at all
*omnis, -e	all, every
*onus, oneris *n*.	burden, load
*opera, -ae *f*.	work, effort, exertion, might
opimus, -a, -um	abundant, copious, splendid
opinio, opinionis *f*.	opinion, belief, expectation
opinor, opinari, opinatus sum	I think, believe, suppose, imagine
opitulor, opitulari, opitulatus sum	I assist, help, aid
*oportet, oportere, oportuit (*impersonal*)	it is necessary, ought, is right
*oppidum, -i *n*.	town
*opprimo, opprimere, oppressi, oppressum	I press down on, crush, overwhelm
optatus, -a, -um	wished, desired, agreeable, pleasing
optimus, -a, -um (*superlative of* **bonus**)	excellent, best, very good
opto, optare, optavi, optatum	I choose, select, desire
*opus, operis *n*.	work, labour, effort
ordior, ordiri, orsus sum	I begin, commence, make a start
*ordo, ordinis *m*.	order, rank, class
*orno, ornare, ornavi, ornatum	I adorn, decorate, embellish
*oro, orare, oravi, oratum	I beg, entreat

*os, oris *n.*	face, mouth, (*figurative*) eyes
*ostendo, ostendere, ostendi, ostentum	I show, express, demonstrate, exhibit
*palam	openly, publicly
Pallacinus, -a, -um	Palatine, of the Palatine
palma, -ae *f.*	palm branch or wreath, (thus) victory, honour
*parens, parentis *c.*	parent, mother, father
*paro, parare, paravi, paratum	I prepare, get ready
parricidium, -i *n.*	parricide, murder of a father, assassination of a parent
*pars, partis *f.*	part, portion, piece
parum	too little, not enough, insufficiently
*pater, patris *m.*	father
paternus, -a, -um	fatherly, paternal, of a father
*patior, pati, passus sum	I suffer, endure, allow
patrimonium, -i *n.*	inheritance (from a father), patrimony
patrius, -a, -um	paternal, of a father
patronus, -i *m.*	protector, defender, patron
*paucus, -a, -um	little, (*plural*) few
paulus, -a, -um	little, small
*pax, pacis *f.*	peace
peccatum, -i *n.*	fault, error, sin
pecco, peccare, peccavi, peccatum	I err, miss, make a mistake
*pecunia, -ae *f.*	money
penates, penatium *m. pl.*	penates, household gods, gods of the family
penitus	deeply, deep within
*per (+ *accusative*)	through, by means of
perditus, -a, -um	hopeless, desperate, ruined
*perdo, perdere, perdidi, perditum	I destroy, ruin, squander
perfacilis, -e	very easy
perfero, perferre, pertuli, perlatum	I complete, finish, carry through
perfidia, -ae *f.*	faithlessness, treachery
*periculum, -i *n.*	danger, peril
permultus, -a, -um	very much, (*in plural*) very many
pernicies, perniciei *f.*	destruction, ruin, calamity
perraro	very rarely, hardly ever
persona, -ae *f.*	person, character

perspicuus, -a, -um	evident, clear, transparent
*persuadeo, persuadere, persuasi, persuasum (+ *dative*)	I persuade, convince
pertimeo, pertimere, pertimui	I fear greatly, am very afraid
pertineo, pertinere, pertinui	I stretch out, reach towards, relate to, concern
pervolo, pervolare, pervolavi, pervolatum	I fly through, dart, speed through
*pes, pedis *m.*	foot
*peto, petere, petivi, petitum	I seek, ask, beg
pietas, pietatis *f.*	dutiful conduct, devotion, piety
placeo, placere, placui, placitum (*often impersonal*)	I please, am agreeable to
planus, -a, -um	plain, clear, evident
*plenus, -a, -um	full, abundant, rich, plentiful
plures, plura	more
plurimus, -a, -um (*superlative of* multus)	very many
plus	more
poeta, -ae *m.*	poet
*polliceor, polliceri, pollicitus sum	I promise, offer
*populus, -i *m.*	people
porro	moreover, furthermore
portentum, -i *n.*	omen, portent, monstrosity
*posco, poscere, poposci	I demand, beg, request
possessio, possessionis *f.*	possession, seizing, occupying
possideo, possidere, possedi, possessum	I own, possess, am master of
*possum, posse, potui	I am able, can
*post (+ *accusative*)	after
postea quam	after
*postquam	after, when
postremo	finally, at last
postulatio, postulationis *f.*	demand, request, desire
*postulo, postulare, postulavi, postulatum	I ask, demand
*potens, potentis	powerful
*potestas, potestatis *f.*	power, opportunity
potissimum	chiefly, principally, especially
*potius	rather
*praebeo, praebere, praebui, praebitum	I offer, display, show
praeceps, praecipitis	headlong, headfirst

praeclarus, -a, -um	distinguished, remarkable, splendid, excellent
*praeda, -ae *f.*	plunder, spoil
praedium, -i *n.*	farm, estate
praedo, praedonis *m.*	plunderer, robber
praeparo, praeparare, praeparavi, praeparatum	I prepare for, make ready for, make preparations for
praesertim	especially, particularly
*praesidium, -i *n.*	defence, protection
*praesum, praeesse, praefui	I preside over, am at the head of
*praeter (+ *accusative*)	except, besides, beyond
praetereo, praeterire, praeterii, praeteritum	I go by, go past, pass by, pass over
*praetor, praetoris *m.*	praetor, president
primo	first, at first, to begin with
primum	first, at first, to begin with
*primus, -a, -um	first
*pro (+ *ablative*)	for, before, on behalf of
probum, -i *n.*	shameful act, disgraceful act, infamy, shame, reproach
procrastino, procrastinare, procrastinavi, procrastinatum	I put off (until tomorrow), defer, delay
procreo, procreare, procreavi, procreatum	I bring forth, bear, produce, create
procurator, procuratoris *m.*	manager, agent, administrator
prodigium, -i *n.*	portent, prodigy, monster
profecto	actually, truly, assuredly, certainly
profero, proferre, protuli, prolatum	I bring out, bring forward, produce
*proficiscor, proficisci, profectus sum	I set out, depart
profiteor, profiteri, professus	I acknowledge, confess openly
profligo, profligare, profligavi, profligatum	I overthrow, ruin, destroy, finish
prohibeo, prohibere, prohibui, prohibitum	I prevent, hinder, restrain
propinquus, -a, -um	relation, relatives, kinsmen
proprius, -a, -um	one's own, not shared, as private property
*propter (+ *accusative*)	on account of
propterea quod	on account of the fact that, because
propulso, propulsare, propulsavi, propulsatum	I drive back, ward off, repel

prorumpo, prorumpere, prorupi, proruptum	I break forth, rush forth, burst out
proscribo, proscribere, proscripsi, proscriptum	I proscribe, declare an enemy of the state
proscriptio, proscriptionis	proscription (written declaration as a public enemy)
*proximus, -a, -um	nearest, most recent
*publicus, -a, -um	public, state
*pudor, pudoris *m.*	shame, modesty
*pugna, -ae *f.*	fight, battle, combat
*pugno, pugnare, pugnavi, pugnatum	I fight
pulcher, pulchra, pulchrum	fine, beautiful
pungo, pungere, pupugi, punctum	I vex, grieve, trouble, disturb
purgo, purgare, purgavi, purgatum	(legal) I exonerate, clear of a charge, excuse
*puto, putare, putavi, putatum	I think, deem, consider
quadraginta	forty
quadriduum, -i *n.*	four days
*quaero, quarere, quaesivi, quaesitum	I seek, look for, ask
quaeso, quaesere, quaesivi	I beg, ask, entreat
quaestio, quaestionis *f.*	inquiry, investigation, court
quaestus, -us *m.*	gain, profit, advantage
*qualis, -e	of what kind, of such a kind
*quam (+ *superlative*)	as ... as possible, with the greatest ...
*quam (*after comparative*)	than
quam ob rem (*also* quamobrem)	on account of which, for which reason
*quamquam	although, though
quamvis	ever so, however much
*quando	(as question) when? (as indefinite) ever
quantum	how much, to what extent
*quantus, -a, -um	how much, how big, how great
quapropter	on account of which, for which reason
*quasi	as if, as though
*que (*suffix*)	and
quem ad modum	in what manner
*queror, queri, questus sum	I complain, lament, make a complaint
*qui, quae, quod	who, which, what
*qui, quae, quod (+ *subjunctive*)	to, in order to
*quia	since, because

*quidam, quaedam, quoddam	a, a certain
*quidem	indeed
quilibet, quaelibet, quodlibet	anyone, anything
quin	so that ... not, but that, that
quinquaginta	fifty
quippe	certainly, obviously, naturally
*quis, quid	who?, what?
quis, quid	who?, what?
quispiam, quaepiam, quodpiam	someone, anyone
*quisquam, quaequam, quicquam	any, anyone, anybody, anything
*quisque, quaeque, quodque	each, every
*quoad	as far as, as long as
*quod	because
*quod si	but if
*quoniam (+ *subjunctive*)	since (suggesting reason)
*quoque	also
rapina, -ae *f*.	robbery, plundering
raro	rarely, seldom
rarus, -a, -um	rare
*ratio, rationis *f*.	reason, judgement, understanding
recedo, recedere, recessi, recessus	I withdraw, retire
recens, recentis	fresh, new, young, recent
*recipio, recipere, recepi, receptum	I receive, take in, admit, welcome
*rectus, -a, -um	right, correct, proper
recuso, recusare, recusavi, recusatum	I refuse, reject, make an objection
*redeo, redire, redii, reditum	I return, go back
*refero, referre, retuli, relatum	I bring back, turn back, report, announce, mention, record
regio, regionis *f*.	region, neighbourhood
relegatio, relegationis *f*.	banishment, exiling, relegation
relego, relegare, relegavi, relegatum	I send away, send out of the way, remove, relegate
*relinquo, relinquere, reliqui, relictum	I leave behind
*reliquus, -a, -um	rest, remainder
remaneo, remanere, remansi	I stay behind, am left, remain
Remmius, -a, -um	Remmian, relating to the gens Remmia
removeo, removere, removi, remotum	I take away, set aside, remove
reparo, reparare, reparavi, reparatum	I restore, repair

reperio, reperire, repperi, repertum	I find, meet with, find out
reprehendo, reprehendere, reprehendi, reprehensum	I blame, censure, reprove, rebuke
***res, rei** f.*	thing, matter, business
***res publica, rei publicae** f.*	state, republic
***resisto, resistere, restiti**	I resist, withstand, oppose
respiro, respirare, respiravi, respiratum	I breathe
resto, restare, restiti	I stand firm, withstand, hold out
reus, -i *m.*	defendant, the accused
reverto, revertere, reverti	I return, go back
revoco, revocare, revocavi, revocatum	I call back, invite in return
ridiculus, -a, -um	laughable, absurd, ridiculous
Roma, -ae *f.*	Rome
Romanus, -a, -um	Roman
Roscius, -i *m.*	Roscius (the defendant)
***rursus**	again, in turn
***rus, ruris** *n.* (*locative:* **ruri**)	country, countryside, country estate
rusticanus, -a, -um	of the country, rustic
rusticus, -a, -um	rural, rustic, of the countryside
***saepe**	often, frequently
saltem	at least, anyhow
***salus, salutis** *f.*	safety, welfare
***saluto, salutare, salutavi, salutatum**	I greet, pay respects, salute
***sanguis, sanguinis** *m.*	blood
***sapiens, sapientis**	wise, knowing
***sapientia, -ae** *f.*	wisdom, good sense
***satis**	enough, sufficient, satisfactory
scelestus, -a, -um	wicked, accursed
***scelus, sceleris** *n.*	crime, wicked deed
***scio, scire, scivi, scitum**	I know, understand, perceive
Scipiones, -um *m. pl.*	the Scipios (prominent Roman family)
scrupulus, -i *m.*	unease, anxiety, doubt
***se** (*accusative*), **sui**	himself, herself, itself, themselves
***sed**	but, on the contrary, but in fact
sedeo, sedere, sedi, sessum	I sit
***semel**	once
semen, seminis *n.*	seed
***semper**	always, ever

*senatus, -us *m.*	senate
*senex, senis *m.*	old man
*sententia, -ae *f.*	judgement, opinion, sentence
*sentio, sentire, sensi, sensum	I sense, feel, perceive
sepulcrum, -i *n.*	grave, tomb, burial place
*sequor, sequi, secutus sum	I follow, pursue
Servilii, -orum *m. pl.*	the Servilii (prominent Roman family)
servio, servire, servivi, servitum	I devote myself to, serve, labour for
*servus, -i *m.*	slave
sese	emphatic form of se
severitas, severitatis *f.*	seriousness, gravity, sternness, severity
severus, -a, -um	severe, harsh
sex	six
Sex. (*abbreviation*)	Sextus
sexagiens	six million sestertii
*si	if
*sic	so, thus, in this way
sicarius, -i *m.*	assassin, murderer, cutthroat
sicut	as, just as
significo, significare, significavi, significatum	I make known, indicate, show, point out
*similis, -e (+ *genitive*)	like, resembling, similar
*simul	as soon as, at the same time, at the moment
sin	but if, if not
*sine (+ *ablative*)	without
singularis, -e	singular, unique, extraordinary
societas, societatis *f.*	fellowship, alliance, conspiracy
*soleo, solere, solitus sum	I am accustomed, tend to
solitudo, solitudinis *f.*	isolation, desolation
*solum	alone, only
*solus, -a, -um	alone, only
*solvo, solvere, solutus sum	I loose, free, complete, fulfil
*soror, sororis *f.*	sister
spargo, spargere, sparsi, sparsum	I scatter, cast, sprinkle
*specto, spectare, spectavi, spectatum	I look at, watch, gaze upon
splendidus, -a, -um	magnificent, illustrious, distinguished
*spero, sperare, speravi, speratum	I hope, expect
*spolia, -orum *n. pl.*	spoils, booty

Vocabulary

*statim	at once, immediately
stimulo, stimulare, stimulavi, stimulatum	I goad, torment, trouble
studiosus, -a, -um	eager, zealous, favourable, devoted
*studium, -i *n.*	enthusiasm, zeal, exertion, attention
suavis, -e	pleasant, sweet, agreeable
subeo, subire, subii, subitum	I undergo, submit, endure
subsellium, -i *n.*	bench
subsum, subesse	I am under, lie under, lurk in, am concealed in
succurro, succurrere, succurri, succursum	I run to help, assist
suffero, sufferre, sustuli, sublatum	I take on, undertake, bear
suffringo, suffringere (*defective*)	I break
Sulla, -ae *m.*	Sulla (former dictator of Rome)
*sum, esse, fui	I am
*summus, -a, -um	highest, greatest
*sumo, sumere, sumpsi, sumptum	(of orationes) I cite, quote, mention as proof
*supero, superare, superavi, superatum	I rise above, am superior, surpass
supplicium, -i *n.*	punishment, penalty, torture
*suscipio, suscipere, suscepi, susceptum	I undertake, take on, begin
suspicio, suspicionis *f.*	suspicion, distrust
suspiciosus, -a, -um	suspicious, full of suspicion
*suus, sua, suum	his, her, its, their
T. (*abbreviation*)	Titus
tabula, -ae *f.*	board, record
taceo, tacere, tacui, tacitum	I am silent, I say nothing
*talis, -e	such, of such a kind
*tam	so, so much, to such a degree
*tamen	however, nevertheless
tametsi	though, although
*tandem	at last, finally
*tango, tangere, tetigi, tactum	I touch, border on
tantum modo (*phrase*)	only, merely
*tantus, -a, -um	of such size, so great
*telum, -i *n.*	weapon, spear, javelin
temere	rashly, thoughtlessly
tempto, temptare, temptavi, temptatum	I try, attempt, test

*tempus, temporis *n.*	time
*teneo, tenere, tenui, tentum	I hold, hold back, keep, restrain, detain
tenuis, -e	(of people) insignificant, common, of low status
*terror, terroris *m.*	fear, dread, alarm
testis, testis *c.*	witness
Tiberis, Tiberis *m.*	the River Tiber
*timeo, timere, timui	I fear, am afraid of
*timor, timoris *m.*	fear, dread
tiro, tironis *m.*	new recruit, novice, beginner
*tollo, tollere, sustuli, sublatum	I lift, raise, do away with, remove
*tot (*indeclinable*)	so many, such a number of
*totus, -a, -um	whole, entire
*trado, tradere, tradidi, traditum	I hand over, give over
tres, tria	three
tribulis, -is *m.*	man of the same tribe, fellow tribesman
tribunal, tribunalis *n.*	tribunal, raised platform for magistrates
tris (*alternative form of* tres)	three
trucido, trucidare, trucidavi, trucidatum	I cut to pieces, slaughter, butcher
*tu, tui	you (*singular*)
tueor, tueri, tutus sum	I look upon, look after, care for
*tum	then
*tumultus, -us *m.*	disturbance, disorder
turpis, -e	base, disgraceful, shameful
*tuus, -a, -um	your, your's (*singular*)
*ullus, -a, -um	any
Umbria, -ae *f.*	Umbria (a region in central Italy)
*umquam	ever, at any time
*unde	from where?
*undique	from all sides, from every quarter
unicus, -a, -um	only, sole
unus, -a, -um (*genitive:* unius)	one
*urbs, urbis *f.*	city
*usque	as far as, all the way to
*usus, -us *m.*	practice, exercise, association, intimacy
*ut (+ *indicative*)	as, when
*ut (+ *subjunctive*)	that, so that, to, in order to
utilis, -e	useful, beneficial, advantageous

*utor, uti, usus sum (+ *ablative*)	I use, make use of, employ, (of people) am intimate with
*utrum	whether
vacuus, -a, -um	empty, vacant
*valeo, valere, valui, valitum	I am strong, have power, am effective, am valid
*vehementer	violently, strongly, forcibly
Veiens, Veientis	Veian, of Veii (an Etruscan city)
*vel	or even, if you will, or rather, or indeed
*velut	just like, just as
venditio, venditionis *f.*	selling, sale
vendo, vendere, vendidi, venditum	I sell
venia, -ae *f.*	indulgence, kindness, mercy
*venio, venire, veni, ventum	I come
*verbum, -i *n.*	word, expression, discourse
vere	truly, really, properly, rightly
verisimilis, -e	probable, likely, apparently true
veritas, veritatis *f.*	truth, reality
*vero	in truth, in fact, indeed, certainly
versor, versari, versatus sum	I go about, move around, come around
verum	but
verum etiam ...	but also
verum, -i *n.*	truth, reality
*vester, vestra, vestrum	your, yours (*plural*)
vestigium, -i *n.*	track, trace, mark, vestige
*vetus, veteris	old, long-standing
vicinitas, vicinitatis *f.*	neighbourhood, area, vicinity
vicinus, -i *m.*	neighbour
*victoria, -ae *f.*	victory, success
videlicet	one may see, clearly, plainly, evidently
*video, videre, vidi, visum	I see
*videor, videri, visus sum	I seem
*villa, -ae *f.*	house, farm, country-house
*vinco, vincere, vici, victum	I conquer, defeat, overcome, get the better of
vindico, vindicare, vindicavi, vindicatum	I punish, take vengeance on, avenge
*vir, viri *m.*	man
*virtus, virtutis *f.*	goodness, virtue, excellence

*vis (*accusative:* vim, *plural:* vires)	strength, force
*vita, -ae *f.*	life
vitium, -i *n.*	(moral) fault, crime, vice
*vito, vitare, vitavi, vitatum	I avoid, evade
*vivo, vivere, vixi, victum	I live, am alive
*vivus, -a, -um	alive, living
vociferatio, vociferatione *f.*	loud calling, clamour, outcry, declamation
vociferor, vociferari, vociferatus sum	I cry out, I exclaim
*voco, vocare, vocavi, vocatum	I call
Volaterrae, -arum *f.*	Volaterra (a town in Etruria)
*volo, velle, volui	I want, wish
voltus, -us *m.* (*alternative:* vultus)	face, expression, look
voluntas, voluntatis *f.*	wish, will, desire
vos, vestrum / vestri	you (*plural*)